D0486644

A Putting Anger in Its Place

ANNIE CHAPMAN

HARVEST HOUSE PUBLISHERS
Eugene, Oregon 97402

Unless otherwise indicated, Scripture verses are taken from the New American Standard Bible, © 1960, 1962, 1963, 1968, 1971, 1972, 1973, 1975, 1977, 1995 by The Lockman Foundation. Used by permission.

Scripture verses marked NIV are taken from the Holy Bible: New International Version®. NIV®. Copyright © 1973, 1978, 1984 by the International Bible Society. Used by permission of Zondervan Publishing House. The "NIV" and "New International Version" trademarks are registered in the United States Patent and Trademark Office by International Bible Society.

Scripture verses marked KJV are taken from the King James Version of the Bible.

Verses marked NKJV are taken from the New King James Version, Copyright © 1979, 1980, 1982 by Thomas Nelson, Inc., Publishers. Used by permission.

Cover by Paz Design Group, Salem, Oregon

PUTTING ANGER IN ITS PLACE
Copyright © 2000 by Annie Chapman
Published by Harvest House Publishers
Eugene, Oregon 97402

Library of Congress Cataloging-in-Publication Data

Chapman, Annie.
    Putting anger in its place / Annie Chapman.
        p. cm.
    ISBN 0-7369-0442-5
    1. Christian women—Religious life. 2. Anger—Religious aspects—Christianity. I. Title.
BV4527.C465 2000
241'.3—dc21   00-024149

Printed in the United States of America.

01 02 03 04 05 06 07 08 09 / RDP-PT / 10 9 8 7 6 5 4 3

Contents

Acknowledgments

I'm grateful to have the opportunity to thank those who have made this work possible. It is more for the benefit and cleansing of my soul as the writer to admit the help I have received from others than it is for them to read it. For without a doubt, this book would not exist had it not been for the help and influence of those individuals in my life who have patiently endured my arduous journey from anger and toward wholeness.

Most assuredly, I have offended and vented on those who are closest to me, and yet they have graciously acted as though I *am* what God will someday make me *be*.

To my siblings Alice, Ney, Clarence, Becky, and Gayle. I hope we can always be close.

To my children, Nathan and Heidi. Thank you for loving me and thinking the best of me, even when I allowed anger to twist me and get me offtrack. No mother could have sweeter, more devoted children. I am indeed blessed.

To Steve, my husband, friend, business partner, editor, and yokefellow in Christ. We both know this book would be a muddled, incoherent pile of words without your patient gift of "putting the puzzle together." I owe you big time, and it will be my pleasure to spend the rest of my life repaying my debt to you. (It's been a terrific 25 years with you; I can hardly wait for the next 25.)

Thank you, Harvest House Publishers, for getting this book into the hands of the readers.

Pastor Jeff Wickwire (pastor of the University Chapel, Fort Worth, Texas), your pastoral and teaching "thumbprint" is evident from the lifechanging messages I ingest weekly through your taped sermons. God has used you to make a difference in my ability to manage anger.

Many thanks to the women who have graciously shared their stories with me. It is always a risk to confide in an author. You never know where you'll read about your most-guarded secrets. But thank you for trusting me by revealing your hearts. Your stories are sometimes painful, sometimes hilarious, but always honest and helpful. Thank you for being willing to be broken and fed to the masses. God bless you.

Most importantly, thank You, Dear Lord, for being our example of love-filled, selfless giving and abundant, healing forgiveness. Without Your work in my life, I would not be.

Simply devoted to Christ,
Annie Chapman

Foreword

by Steve Chapman

As the ladies came into the church through the double glass doors, the winter wind blew the flying snow into the foyer. While it was a bitter cold Saturday morning on the outside, I knew that each of the women attending this event would feel the warmth of a welcome as the hostesses from the church greeted them with directions to the coffee, tea, and pastries. There was an excitement in the air as the ladies hung coats and scarves on the hallway hangers and turned with a smile toward the cafeteria.

I was there as an assistant to my wife, Annie, who had been invited to speak at this day planned just for women. One of my tasks was to prepare the stage for sound and oversee the technical side of the event. As I went about my duties, the ladies began to make their way into the sanctuary. I observed how pleasant they seemed. Each one was cordial and polite as she found a seat and quietly conversed with her friends in the pews. I thought about the husbands, children, and loved ones each woman represented, and on that blustery winter day my heart was warmed by the scene. I was grateful that Annie would have the opportunity to share her heart with a group like the one that was filling the auditorium.

When Annie began her presentation, I turned to another of my tasks—making sure a questionnaire was placed on the table that displayed her books. She announced that the form was there and requested that each lady consider answering the questions. The title of the inquiry was "Women and Anger." Annie made it clear that she was seeking responses to the questions as an aid to her book project on the issue. When the first session ended, I was amazed to see how eager the ladies were to get a copy of the questionnaire. They disappeared to different parts of the church, keeping pencils and pens busy.

When Annie and I said our good-byes that day and we headed down the highway on our return trip to Tennessee, little did I know the levels of pain that had been inscribed on those pieces of paper. The ladies I had seen at that conference appeared so affable and good-natured on the outside. But after hearing Annie read with tears their anonymous cries regarding the anger that filled their souls, I wondered how so many of them could carry such pain in their hearts. It was an eye-opener for me.

However, Annie was not surprised. For quite some time she had been studying the Scriptures and other helpful resources in an effort to extend a helping hand to women who deal with the emotion of anger. Her purpose in gathering the questionnaires was to confirm some of the revelations she had encountered during her research. And the forms the ladies had completed had done just that. While Annie may not have been caught off-guard by the responses on the paper, I couldn't help but recall how shocking it was that underneath the smiles and finery of the outward appearance of the ladies I had seen, there was a seething anger ready to explode in so many of them.

As a foreword to this book that Annie has openly and care-fully penned, some of the questions that were on that form are listed on the next page. Along with them are some of the responses gleaned from the group on that winter day. Perhaps in them you will recognize some of the emotions these ladies deal with. If they sound hauntingly familiar, then the reading of the pages that follow will be of help to you. Later on, by the way, you will again come to this list of questions. Room is provided in the book for you to answer them as well.

Women and Anger Questionnaire

1. **When was the last time you were angry?**

    Last night
    Yesterday
    2 days ago
    Every day
    Consistent
    Several weeks ago when my husband broke confidence
    again!

2. **How did you express this anger?**

    Silent treatment
    Cried
    Threw something
    Cold shoulder
    By yelling and walking away
    Short sentences, body language
    Yelled and told my kids I hate them and they are
    ungrateful
    Vented!

Tongue lashing and treating my husband like a child
Screaming
Yelled at my 3-year-old daughter
Silent until I cried uncontrollably
Glared
Hitting
Cursing!
Withheld sex

3. Who received the brunt of your anger?

A friend, because nobody was listening at home
The people I love most
Kids, husband
My kids and their friends
Myself, because I withdrew
My fiancé
The object I threw
My coworker
My mother
Anyone in my way
Everyone!

4. On a scale of 1-10, with "1" being only mildly irritated and "10" being out of your mind with rage, where do you generally live?

(Of the nearly 200 forms completed, the average on the scale was an "8." Very few were a "1" or "2.")

5. On what occasion did you experience anywhere near a "10"?

A week ago I was sick, the kids wouldn't take a nap, and I threw one of their toys and sent them to their rooms.

At the beginning of our marriage.

Found my husband on the Internet with porn and my boys walked in and saw it. (There were several women who mentioned husbands involved with pornography.)

Road rage: When a car with a young couple and a child passed me on double yellow lines and made oncoming cars swerve off the road. I tailgated them. I was wrong and needed God's forgiveness!

When kids keep asking the same questions and doing the same wrong things.

When my father betrayed me when I was 16.

I mistreated my children, but I knew it stemmed from something that happened in my early childhood.

When my husband told me he spent money on something unnecessary without the two of us agreeing on it. He didn't acknowledge that we had bills to pay. Also, when he watches other women and pays no attention to me.

When my husband lied to me about going to strip joints.

During a divorce.

My boyfriend (at the time) and I sinned together and I was mad at myself and him for not saying anything about it.

When my daughter was seeing a young man we did not approve of.

When my husband committed a crime that sent him to prison for five years.

When I can't finish something.

My nephew killed my parents and pled innocent.

---

6. To whom do you owe an apology?

My husband
My children
My mother and her friends
Myself
A coworker
A cousin
My in-laws
Everybody
God

Obviously, these responses represent the most intense feelings written. Not all the ladies wrote that they lived at the "boiling point," and some even admitted they had dealt with anger and it was no longer the struggle it had once been in their lives. That was encouraging to us. However, since that day, the questionnaire has made even more rounds, and the truth is disturbing. Far too many women have expressed exactly what is recorded above. It is for that reason that I commend Annie for diving into the dangerous waters of this issue and being willing to be used by the Lord as a reminder that He alone is the rescuer. I know her well, and I can confidently assure you that she continues to effectively deal with this challenge in her own life.

As a husband, I have benefited greatly by God's work in Annie. Our children, Nathan and Heidi, have been blessed as well. And, as a parting word, I rejoice in knowing that if this is an issue you battle, those around you will be grateful that you will have invested some valuable time in learning how to put anger in its place.

The Answer to Anger

It seemed as though it took days to drive the 400 miles from Nashville, Tennessee, to the all-too-familiar hospital where my mother had been taking chemotherapy treatments for nearly 10 years. But this trip home was not like all the others. I was not driving home to take Mom to the doctor and spend a day or two visiting with my parents. No, this was a different kind of visit. This was a journey I had dreaded and one for which I was totally unprepared. The cancer had taken its ultimate revenge on Mom's overworked, tired, and thin body.

After I arrived, I spent the next few hours at her bedside as my father sat beside her and lovingly patted and stroked her bony hand. For 52 years they had worked side by side, striving to raise six children and forge out a living on a small dairy farm. But this night there was one final job left for them to do together. Mom had to trudge through the painful task of letting go of her diseased body, while grabbing hold of life on the other side. They would do it together, as they had done every other job they encountered during their long marriage.

The remaining children drove through the night, and by early morning all six of us were gathered around her, not unlike a mother hen and her little chicks. It would not be until later in the day that the dreadful deed would be accomplished. There were tears of love and words of comfort, and my sister Rebecca softly read Proverbs 31 to Mom as she walked through the door of eternity.

I came back to my childhood home from the hospital after she died. My mother's passing had changed me, and I could sense it immediately. It was strange to walk into the house without receiving the expected—and cherished—hugs and kisses from my mother. Everything seemed hollow and surreal. As I looked around at the familiar surroundings, I began to see things I had overlooked before. Even the smallest items took on a new and special meaning, like the grocery list I found that Mom had written on the back of an empty envelope. Because she had touched it, it became an instant treasure. As the waves of memories washed over me, I realized that all we ever truly leave behind when we are gone is what people remember of us. I determined that day to frequently reassess the memory I would eventually become in the minds and hearts of those I love.

There's an old story about a grandchild sitting with his grandfather. The grandfather was a rough old fellow with little patience for anyone. The grandson says, "Grandpa, make a sound like a frog."

Irritated, the grandfather responds with an abrupt, "No!"

The grandson persistently asks again, "Please, Grandpa, make a sound like a frog."

The grandson receives the same answer, only this time with an even more gruff "No!" The child pleads one more time, "Please?"

Finally, the grandfather asks the boy, "Why do you want me to make a sound like a frog?"

The boy responds, " 'Cause Grandma says, 'When Grandpa croaks, we can all go to Six Flags.'"

While that little tale has its element of humor, there's a sobering revelation generated by it. Proverbs 10:7 says, "The memory of the righteous is blessed, but the name of the wicked will rot." That passage compels me to ask myself some serious questions. *What will my family remember about me? What are the words they will use to describe me?*

There are some wonderful things I'd like my family and those I love to be able to say about me. I would hope they could say that, like my own mother, I was patient, kind, honest, and a lover of things like the medicine of good, clean humor. These, among other delightful attitudes, are what I long for them to recall when they mention my name.

On the other hand, there are some things for certain I *don't* want them to say about me after I am gone. I wouldn't want it said that I was manipulative, stubborn, or sour. May it never be! And at the very top of the list of descriptions offered about me, there are five words I sincerely pray can never be uttered to identify me: *She was an angry woman.* To think that I would be remembered as a sharp-tongued, bitter person who always had to be right and always had to have her own way would be nothing less than tragic.

Realizing that anger can be a vicious destroyer of one's good memory in the minds of others, I determined to make some changes in my life. As I stood in the quiet of my mother's house, I made a decision that would eventually alter my very character. I set my sights on controlling and conquering my nature to display rage and to pray for the reward of leaving a legacy that my loved ones could point to with a smile.

The following pages are the result of that battle with the enemy called anger and the eventual discovery of the source of victory. They are written to assist women who, like me, have been known to give anger a home. I spent most of my growing-up years feeling like a volcano, ripe to erupt at the least provocation. The journey away from anger and toward peace has been a long and difficult road, but one I am glad to have pursued these many years.

I know I am not alone in this war against anger and a quest for peace. Many of you also wrestle with this plaguing problem. I know because you have told me so. It manifests itself in bizarre ways. For instance, a woman whose 21-year-old daughter was murdered while attending college was fiercely angry at her sister when she didn't call on the birthday of her deceased child. The wounded mother was tempted to cut off all ties with her sister, even though it had been that very sibling who had been a rock of support during the days following the murder. The mother was furious because of the perceived insensitivity she felt her sister had shown by failing to recognize the niece's birthday.

What was the real problem? The mother chose anger as the emotion of choice, rather than facing the debilitating grief that shrouded her day. Perhaps she chose anger because it appeared to empower, while grief made her feel vulnerable. There are times when anger seems far more manageable than sadness.

In another situation, a mother whose son had left behind the godly teaching given to him in his childhood in order to pursue a lifestyle of homosexuality was constantly in a state of anger. At whom was her anger directed? She didn't really know; she just knew that at any given moment she would reach the "boiling point." And nothing more than the slightest inconvenience would spark the blazing fires of anger. This mother, disappointed with her child and disappointed with God for letting him stray, was mad at the devil for being the killer and destroyer of all things good. She was so confused she didn't know with *whom* she was angry. She just knew she was tormented.

Still another woman watched as her mother died a slow, excruciating death. It was a painful dying that medicine could not numb. She watched as her mother writhed in agony, longing for relief that did not come quickly. This woman knew exactly where her anger was directed. She was infuriated with God. She told me, "I have served God for nearly forty years. I have loved Him and trusted Him with every area of my life. However, I can't get my mother's cries for help out of my mind. I am so angry that God let her suffer in this way. But, after two years of these resentful feelings toward God, I am in real need of relief. I'm tired of being angry."

This troubled woman went on to say how disappointed her mother would have been if she knew the depth of her daughter's anger against God that had spanned two long years. She wept as she said, "My mother trusted God with all her heart. She would never have wanted me to let her death come between me and the God she loved so deeply."

Women and anger seem to go together. Perhaps it is in line with our jobs as nurturers—there are just so many irritations to encounter, so much responsibility to shoulder, and so little energy to handle it all. I remember the time that a popular television personality was voted Mother of the Year. It galled me when I read in a magazine that the woman was working two full-time television shows and had around-the-clock nannies. I thought, "Well, I could be Mother of the Year, too, if I never had to be around my children." I know it sounds like I live on a diet of sour grapes and lemon juice, but hey, that TV celebrity does not represent most of us. I would dare say that very few ladies on this busy planet have nonstop servants who help with their fast-paced lives. Most of us would have been much better qualified for the award. No one knows just how nice and sweet I can be when I'm not bothered by people who irritate me and demand from me. The truth is, the only time I'm really hard to live with is when I have to interact with humans or things.

Anger in the life of a woman is inevitable, but it's a problem that can and must be managed. Controlling it and keeping it from crossing the line into sin is a process worthy of our time and attention. Be encouraged. There is an answer to the overwhelming, paralyzing effect and power of anger in the life of a woman.

1

Starting Down the Road from Rage

"We know that all things work together for good to those who love God, to those who are the called according to His purpose."

—ROMANS 8:28 (NKJV)

I was born in rural West Virginia and raised on a dairy farm as the fourth of six children. I remember when I was five years old, a preacher came to our house. We were an unchurched family at the time, and so it was a big deal to have a minister come visit, and an especially big deal to a little, dirty-faced, barefooted child.

I have a vivid recollection of going into the house with my mother and the preacher. Mom disappeared into the kitchen to get him a glass of water. While she was gone the preacher did two things that would change my life forever. First of all, he showed me the classic picture of Jesus knocking at the door. Second, he told me something I would never forget. He pointed to the picture of Jesus and said to me, a little poor kid, "That man loves you." I clearly remember thinking, "Well, if that man loves me, then I love Him!" I was totally unaware that I was fulfilling 1 John 4:19 that says, "We love, because He first loved us."

The knowledge of Christ's love for me would become a life rope to which I would desperately cling in the days that followed. I have no doubt that in God's divine providence, He orchestrated the visit by the preacher in the early summer for the express purpose of assuring me of Jesus' love and care for me. By the end of that same season, I was cruelly raped by a farmhand who worked for my father. That violent, criminal act changed everything for me. There was great damage done to my ability to trust anyone, making the years that followed very difficult. At that time no one around me understood the long-range effect of such an assault. All of the adults, especially the ones in the court system, assumed that because I was a child I would forget what had happened. Of course, as some of you know far too well, one never forgets. There was no one to whom I could talk, no one to help me work through the anger and confusion.

The effect of my seething rage was manifested in a morbid yet earnest desire to die. I remember that as an elementary-school child and on into my teen years, I would sit on the hillside behind our farm and pray for God to take my life. Time and time again I would beg, "If there is a God, then kill me. Don't make me live with this sadness inside of me." I could identify with the despair found in Job 3:20,21. "Why is light given to him who suffers, and life to the bitter of soul; who long for death, but there is none, and dig for it more than for hidden treasure." I would wait for God to answer my prayer and when I didn't die, I would get up disappointedly and go home, only to return and offer the same desperate prayer on another day.

In all actuality, it felt like death was living inside of me. Over the years I have talked to many women who have experienced the same type of overwhelming desire for death in order to end emotional suffering. If a long, sustained anger has robbed you and you don't want to live, let me assure you, there is someone you can go to who will help you experience freedom from that debilitating way of thinking. His name is Jesus.

For me, it wasn't until I was 18 years old that I finally heard the rest of the story about Him. I learned that not only did Jesus love me, but He loved me enough to die for me. When I was a freshman in college, I made the "great exchange." I gave Jesus my desire to die, and He gave me His life. Along with that new life, He gave me a sincere longing to be free from the anger and bitterness that held me captive.

The very day I gave my heart and life to Christ, I began a journey that continues to this day. While my life became a spiritual bed of roses as I began to rest in Him, there were still the emotional thorns that had to be removed. Christ was living in me, but I still had to deal with the years of having nursed a gaping, infected, wounded heart as well as destructive thought patterns. Dealing with the persistent anger that resulted from being wounded so deeply has been an extreme challenge in my life, and yet the work that Christ has done in my heart and mind has been worth the difficult journey.

There were many roads I could have taken that would have led me away from rage. Self-help groups, counting to 10, taking a cold shower, beating a couch with a baseball bat, and even primal therapy might have offered a temporary fix. However, to find a lasting solution, I had no better choice than to entrust my life to the God who made me.

I'll admit that to some, yielding my life to God, trusting Him to allow only those things that will work to my good (Romans 8:28), seems childishly simplistic, especially in light of my painful situation. And for me to suggest to them this same path to freedom may not only sound simplistic, but even offensively insensitive. But believe me, while it sounds elementary, in no way whatsoever is it easy!

To illustrate this, if you have ever experienced an excruciating toothache, you might have been upset when some well-meaning person casually suggested, "You just need to go to the dentist and have the offending tooth pulled out." While their advice is uncomplicated, you know very well that taking your hurting tooth to someone who is going to ream and gouge on it is not, by any means, an easy chore. Your painful ordeal may be over in just a matter of moments as the dentist extracts and discards the rotten tooth, but no one can tell you it was a walk in the park.

To carry this analogy a littler further, let's assume your tooth has complications that require much more attention. Before the dentist can pull your tooth, you may have to be placed on a series of medications to fight back an abscess. No dentist worth his salt will do a root canal or even a simple extraction if there is infection present. Ultimately, the dentist might pull the tooth, but in the meantime he must first deal with the foul problem.

For some of us, the road from rage may be a simple procedure, like the extraction of a tooth. The pain is real, but comparatively minimal and quickly resolved. However, for others, the healing requires much more work from hands of "The Great Physician." And, it requires a great deal more from the patient. Seeking God to discover where the rage started, identifying the offending people who must be forgiven (or asked for forgiveness), confessing the sin to God, forsaking it, and going about the hard work of reprogramming the thought processes are all part of the procedure. Sound simple? Yes, perhaps it does sound doable. But is it easy? Absolutely not! Battling thought patterns, humbling ourselves and dying to the human pride that got us to the point of trying to live independently from God, and receiving His grace to deal with the predicament are never easy. Nevertheless, I have discovered that getting free from anger and striving for a heart that is ready and willing to forgive have changed my life, given me reason to live, and taught me the true purpose for my existence.

Romans 8:28, mentioned earlier, is a familiar passage that we often quote when something terrible has happened to us. No matter how tragic the situation is in our own hearts and minds, we can tell ourselves that, "…we know that God causes all things to work together for good to those who love God, to those who are called according to His purpose." Verse 29 tells us what that purpose is: "For whom He foreknew, He also predestined to become conformed to the image of His Son…" From that declaration, I can trust that absolutely nothing, including that which has stirred up a fierce anger, can touch me without first passing through the filter of His loving hands. If something that I perceive as horrible enters my life, I must lean on Him to be my strength, my deliverer, and I must look for the good in it that will make me more like Christ. As strange as it sounds to say, I can rejoice that I have been made worthy of suffering.

Modern Western Christianity too often teaches that the most important thing in our life is to be happy, wealthy, and healthy. However, all we have to do is look back in church history to find that "sharing in the sufferings of Christ" is the norm. In fact, we are instructed in 1 Peter 4:12 that we are not even supposed to be surprised when difficulties find us: "Beloved, do not be surprised at the fiery ordeal among you, which comes upon you for your testing, as though some strange thing were happening to you; but to the degree that you share the sufferings of Christ, keep on rejoicing; so that also at the revelation of His glory, you may rejoice with exultation." In the text, Peter was writing to Christians who were living in a pagan culture that did not understand or appreciate the One true God. As a result of that culture's mindset, the Christians were being persecuted and martyred for the cause of Christ. In verse 19 it goes on to say, "Therefore, let those also who suffer according to the will of God *entrust* their souls to a faithful Creator in doing what is right" (emphasis mine). The word "entrust" in this verse is also used as the word "commit" that Jesus spoke from the cross as He prayed, "Father, into Thy hands, I *commit* My spirit" (Luke 23:46, emphasis mine). Even Christ found it a great challenge to entrust His life into the hands of the Heavenly Father. Yet, we are privileged to follow Him in this glorious opportunity. And it comes to us in the form of suffering.

Only in America are we taught that God will not withhold any desire or degree of happiness from us. This teaching and way of thinking is totally contrary to what is truly important in our lives. It is not our momentary happiness and fulfillment that is paramount, but God wants to use everything that comes into our lives to conform us into the image of Jesus. As long as we hold on to things like anger, and our right to be correct and accommodated, we will never experience the progress we desire.

Like the loaves and the fishes that were broken and shared with the masses in order to feed the hungering souls, we too must be willing to be broken and poured out for the purposes of God. When I started writing this book, I did not intend to be so candid with my own life and struggles. However, the more I studied, the more I realized that sharing my own failures and brokenness was the only way to make this book helpful to others. I want to offer to you the things I have learned as a woman who has trudged down the long road of healing, and perhaps I may guide you to God "who makes all things new"! It is from this background that I respectfully suggest to you that His hands be allowed to operate on your heart. If you will allow Him to do so, you will find that you are on the road *from* rage and on your way to His joy!

2

Anger: The Emotional "Lint Trap"

"But seek first His kingdom and His righteousness; and all these things shall be added to you."

—MATTHEW 6:33

Why is it so hard to admit when we are feeling angry? I recently spoke with a friend whose husband of 25 years had left her. She had been replaced by a woman 20 years her junior. The public humiliation was horrible. No one could believe that *he* would do such a terrible thing to his family. As we talked, I asked, "Are you angry with your husband?" Her response was, "No, I'm not angry. I'm just hurt."

However, she went on to describe what his adulterous actions had done to the children, the church, and his entire family. All the emotions she described were "angry" feelings, and yet she could not admit that it was anger she was experiencing. Perhaps it was not an unwillingness to admit her ire, but an inability to distinguish between the various emotional feelings that transpire.

Acknowledging to ourselves that we are angry sounds pretty simple. However, some of us have a very hard time doing it because we have been taught that being angry is wrong. Anger in itself is not a sin. If it were, God would have to be considered a sinner. In the Old Testament the word "anger" is used 455 times, and of those times 375 instances refer to God being angry. Psalm 7:11 says, "God is angry with the wicked every day" (NKJV). Our ability to be angry demonstrates the thumbprint of our Creator on our lives. We are made in the image of God, and part of His character is the capability to be angry at wickedness, injustice, and the molestation of truth.

Dr. Gary Chapman states in his book *The Other Side of Love*, "Anger, then, is the emotion that arises whenever we encounter what we perceive to be wrong. The emotional, physiological, and cognitive dimensions of anger leap to the front burner of our experience when we encounter injustice."[1]

The following questions may help us define our struggle with anger. As you read and answer these questions, it is imperative that you be honest with yourself. It may be a comfort to understand that experiencing anger is not the issue; it is how we handle anger that is the challenge.

1. When was the last time you were angry?

2. How did you express this anger?

3. Who received the brunt of your expressed anger?

4. On a scale of 1-10, with "1" being only mildly irritated and "10" being out of your mind with rage, where do you generally live?

5. On what occasion did you experience anywhere near a "10"?

6. Who has received the majority of your angry outbursts?

7. To whom do you owe an apology?

8. Who has offended you and not yet apologized?

9. What is a typical expression of your anger (throwing things, cursing, hitting, kicking, sulking, silent treatment, pouting)?

10. Name two things that would be helpful in freeing you from the negative results of anger.

These questions were not intended to be an exhaustive exploration of angry feelings. You may find another way to pinpoint and define anger in your life. Regardless of the instrument of discovery you use, it will be helpful to recognize anger for what it is and then take steps to control it more effectively. Let me say it again: The bad news is that anger is one of those problems that cannot be cured. The good news is that it *can* be managed.

We are human beings and it is in our nature, from our very beginning, to put our own needs and concerns first in the line of attention. Years ago our pastor shared with us a description of the human plight. See if it sounds familiar.

Every baby starts life as a little savage. He is completely selfish and self-centered. He wants what he wants, when he wants it: his bottle, his mother's attention, his playmates' toys, his uncle's watch. Deny these wants and he seethes with rage and aggressiveness. He would be murderous if he were not so helpless. He is dirty, he has no morals, no knowledge, no developed skills. This means that all children are born delinquent. If permitted to continue in their self-compulsive actions to satisfy each want, every child would grow up a criminal, killer and a rapist.

The sobering truth about this quote is that it was taken from The Minnesota Crime Commission.

Why do we have such an ongoing struggle with anger? Because anger is a natural reaction that arises when we don't get our way. Not all anger is borne of a desire to serve self. There are situations when we can justifiably be "righteously indignant." However, I suspect the anger that gets us in the most trouble is not at all as righteous as we might think.

God's anger is different from human anger. His wrath is controlled. It is not selfish, and its expression is always for the concern of others. The purpose of godly anger is to correct or stop destructive behavior and to be an expression of love and concern. God's anger is directed at broken relationships, injustice, and willful disobedience.

In contrast, human anger is uncontrolled and lacking patience. Ecclesiastes 7:9 says, "Do not be eager in your heart to be angry, for anger resides in the bosom of fools." Human anger is borne of an appetite for revenge, to hurt those who offended, to destroy individuals, and it is only concerned with self-preservation.

In order to understand if our anger is a form of "righteous anger," look at the following sentences and see if the statements are true.

I feel anger...

...when I am not valued as a person.

...when my husband ignores me.

...when my kids don't pick up their rooms.

...when the traffic light does not change quickly.

...when someone cuts in front of me on the highway or in the grocery line.

...when I have to wait in line for any reason.

...when the repairman doesn't call back.

...when my plane is late.

...when I get physically injured.

...when I have to take the dog out (again).

...when the phone rings and interrupts me.

...when I eat right and still gain weight.

Each time anger occurs as a result of the above scenarios, notice that it happens when a perceived "personal right" has been violated.

Look at the list again and ask yourself just what "rights" do we have? Do we have the "right" to be valued as a person or loved by a spouse? Do we have the "right" to have cooperative children, to be free from interruptions from red lights, stop signs, speed bumps, construction detours, tardy planes, or traffic accidents? Do we have the "right" to be free from less skillful drivers than ourselves? Do we have the "right" to go to the front of every line, to be shown courtesy, to be free from physical harm or catastrophes? Do we have the "right" to be free from needy people or things? Do we have the "right" to be rewarded for our sacrifices?

Some of these do indeed sound like legitimate needs while others show just how unreasonable humans can be. Even though I have needs and desires, I don't have the "right" to express them in the form of anger. We become angry when our "rights" are violated. So what do we do to rid ourselves of unwanted, uncontrollable anger? We turn our "rights" over to God.

Only when we transfer our "rights" to Him and ask that He meet our basic need to be whole and healthy individuals, will we be free from the never-ending pursuit of trying to claim what we perceive as ours. We all want to be loved and valued. We long for a cooperative family, adequate possessions, and a peaceful life. However, if we seek only those things, we will never truly be satisfied and it is likely that anger will result. Matthew 6:33 points us to our greatest need: "But seek first His kingdom and His righteousness; and all these things shall be added to you." The verses prior to this passage are careful to not ignore the human's basic requirements for existence, such as food, shelter, and clothing. But the clear implication is that our higher needs are spiritual.

Furthermore, Matthew 5:5 says, "Blessed are the meek [the humble, the gentle], for they shall inherit the earth" (NKJV). The opposite of meek (or gentle) is angry (mad or vengeful). The two conflicting emotions cannot coexist in the same heart. Either we will give ourselves over to humility or we will proudly live in anger. We do have a choice.

As Christians we are to live as selfless, stuff-less, gentle souls. Does that sound weak and pitiful to you? I dare say, that is the hardest prescription for living I could ever imagine.

It's Easy to Get Angry!

To illustrate how quickly and easily we can get angry over unfulfilled expectations, consider what happened to my friend Susan. One evening she called ahead to let her family know that she was on her way home from work. A self-employed mother of three, her business was just five minutes from her residence. The call was what could be considered the "two-minute warning." The children assured her the kitchen was clean and the house was picked up. The last thing Susan wanted to do was to walk into the house at ten o'clock at night and start cleaning. Reassured with the promise that all was tended to, she calmly drove home to see her precious family.

When she arrived and entered the house, she was immediately transported from warm and loving feelings toward her loved ones to complete and utter outrage. The kitchen was filled with dishes from breakfast as well as dishes from the remaining day's meals. Nothing had been done! The children and the tired husband were lying around like giant slugs, gazing mindlessly at the hypnotic glare of the television.

Susan was furious that she had been so callously deceived. What was the problem? Susan had worked all day and was tired. All she asked was that the teenage children throw away their own trash, wash the dishes they dirtied, and pick up their own stuff. When she walked into the kitchen and saw the mountain of debris, it was understandable that she was irritated. However, she didn't stay irritated long. No, her annoyance quickly transformed her into "terminator mom." She started throwing whatever item she found that was not in its proper place. The first victim was a Walkman tape recorder. It soon became a dangerous projectile as it flew across the room. (It's amazing how sturdy they make those things!)

She was further outraged when her husband scolded the lazy teenagers by saying, "You should have cleaned the kitchen! Look what you made your mother do." Susan perceived this to be the wrong reaction. Now, Dad was in trouble. She wanted her husband to support her in pointing out *their* wrong behavior, not *hers*. Needless to say, the evening was shot. Everyone was upset by the time they went to bed. The children slunk away to their rooms saying, "What's wrong with Mom?" The husband and wife were at odds because each blamed the other for her outburst of anger.

Everyone in this family was looking out for their own "rights." The teenagers thought they had the "right" to be served by their mother. After all, until just recently, Mom had always been there when they came home from school. They always made a mess, but Mom was there to clean it up. They resented giving up the "right" to be lazy, sloppy children.

Susan's husband thought he had the "right" to come home from a hard day's work and not have to reprimand the kids about how the house looked. He knew from the past that Susan always cleaned it up...eventually. He didn't want the bother of being the "heavy" with the children. He wanted the "right" to be left out of it.

Susan thought she had the "right" to have some help. She had decided to work a demanding job, and she thought it was understood that things were going to change. She expected the rest of the family to sacrifice since she was doing her part. She was angry when she realized she was the only one who had taken on the lion's share of responsibilities.

It looked like the problems in Susan's life were a dirty house and an uncooperative family. But what it really came down to was the same problem it always is when humans deal with anger. Someone's "rights" had been violated. Like the lint trap in a clothes dryer, when all of our unmet expectations gather in one place (our hearts), eventually the machine malfunctions.

3

I Change My Mind— I Don't Want to Be Angry Anymore!

"As far as the east is from the west, so far has He removed our transgressions from us."

—PSALM 103:12

The most dangerous roads I have ever driven on have also been the widest. I remember an interstate in Los Angeles that scared me senseless. It was a five-lane monster. People were darting in and out and back and forth as they flashed down the highway at breakneck speeds. That treacherous interstate reminds me of the five coping mechanisms I experienced as I learned to deal with anger—suppression, visible aggression, hidden aggression, reaching out, and resolution. When I was in each phase of dealing with anger, there were times when I could function quite well. Then there were other times when my everyday life was greatly hindered by my struggle. As you read the following description of each "lane," perhaps you can identify where you are on your journey.

Suppression

There are those who are very skeptical of individuals who claim to have repressed memories. Perhaps it is only after hypnosis or psychological probing that they discover they were molested as a baby or even as an older child. Only when they were under some sort of medical or mental stress did they realize what had happened. There is no way I can know whether someone's accusation is true or false. However, I do understand that the mind has the ability to categorize painful memories and protect a fragile heart from thoughts that are overwhelming.

For many years I had long periods of time when I successfully suppressed the terrible thing that happened to me as a child. In fact, there are large sections of my childhood that are a complete blank to me. I didn't even want to know if the memories would be good or bad. I was quite comfortable with leaving well enough alone. However, as I got older, my memories of the childhood assault became more and more difficult to suppress.

To further explain the danger of refusing to deal with the traumas of our childhood, I will borrow another illustration from the world of dentistry. One day, my dear friend Allison noticed a slight pimple on her gum, right above her front tooth. She picked at the sore place and decided it was just a small, infected blemish. After she "fiddled" with it, it seemed to go away. A couple of weeks later, she discovered the pimple was back. Again, she simply opened the top of the sore and it went away. Months passed and then one day she noticed that not only had the pimple returned, but her tooth was very sore. She finally went to the dentist, and he announced the unwelcome news that Allison's tooth was infected and she needed a root canal.

After a few days on antibiotics, she returned to the dentist to have her tooth fixed.

Six hundred dollars and four hours later, the dentist completed his work. Allison went home but noticed her tooth still hurt quite a lot. In fact, her lip had begun to swell and the side of her face was very tender to the touch. With each passing hour, she got worse and worse. Her eye began to blacken and her face was double the size it should have been. In a panic she called the dentist. She was assured that it was quite normal to be sore after such an invasive procedure. However, she didn't get any better. Finally, Allison went back to the dentist and he closely checked her to see what was wrong.

My friend was very upset to hear that the root of the tooth had cracked and she was going to eventually lose it. As disturbed as she was, it was nothing compared to the continued pain she was suffering. The next day, she went to work, despite looking quite hideous, with her swollen face, turned-up lip, and blackened eye.

She began to cry because of the excruciating pain. As she started to weep, something terrible happened. With the added pressure of her sobbing, she felt her tooth literally explode. She ran to the bathroom and held her mouth over the sink. Out of the place her tooth had been moments before, bitter infection poured into the sink. Horrified at what was happening, she had a coworker call the dentist. Needless to say, Allison was hurried in for emergency dental surgery. Not only did she lose her tooth, but she ran the risk of losing her very life. Her entire sinus cavity was filled with infection. The violent explosion of her tooth was the pressure valve releasing the lethal infection.

Had Allison not ignored the first signs of infection represented by the recurring pimple, perhaps she could have saved her tooth. We won't ever know for sure. In the same way, when we suppress hurts and damage from childhood, it is not only painful, but it can result in tremendous loss and even rob us of our lives.

I was a person literally consumed with hatred and bitter anger because of what someone had done to me. I knew I was not supposed to hate, so I hid my dreadful thoughts from everyone, including God. As long as I refused to be honest with Him, I was sadly destined to be under the power and control of my anger.

Visible Aggression

Even though I was trying to ignore my anger and thus delaying the process of dealing with the root cause for it, there were many times that the pressure valve would blow. Pity the person who got in my way when I was venting my anger. One time that stands out in my memory was an episode with a young boy who was working for my dad. I hated this kid simply because he was another hired farmhand. Although I had no reason to feel such disgust for him personally, it was *who* he represented in my mind that bothered me. I experienced an all-consuming rage toward this poor child who was just trying to make a couple of dollars for his family.

This kid's developmentally disabled elder brother rode the same school bus as me. One morning I was in a foul mood, and everyone could tell. The older brother made an audible and lewd insinuation about his younger brother and me. Without any hesitation or restraint, I open-handedly slapped that poor, retarded boy with every ounce of strength I could muster. I actually uncrossed his crossed eyes for a short time. Needless to say, he never teased me again.

That particular incident is very clearly tucked away in my mind. After I slugged the boy, I realized just how little control I had over my anger. If I had had a gun, I'm fairly certain I would have shot him. There was nothing that could have dampened my rage. I was a pressure cooker, and if I didn't release the steam I was going to turn into a bomb. A few years later, by the way, the same boy who had worked for my dad was killed while working on a river barge. I suffered a lot of guilt over that tragedy, wondering if somehow my hatred had contributed to his death. Anger and unforgiveness had me so locked up, I became a prisoner in my own mind.

Hidden Aggression

By the time I was 12 years old there were some serious physical manifestations of the rage that was trapped inside me. My parents were told that before I reached the age of 21, I would be confined to a wheelchair. I was afflicted with crippling arthritis, and I spent my entire childhood in severe pain. Ben Gay topical ointment and Deep Heating Rub were my mainstays. My arms were so weak and my shoulders were so pain-filled that I couldn't lift them far enough from my sides to dress myself. I missed many days of school in my elementary years because I couldn't get ready to leave the house. At night I would hurry to bed, trying to get to sleep before the pain intensified.

The doctor wanted to put me on tranquilizers. Everyone realized that the root cause of my pain was emotional, yet no one knew how to help me. I refused the medication, and I thank

God that I did. Somehow I knew that if I started taking pills at the age of 12, I'd never be free of them.

I can't help but think of the millions of children today who are being medicated with a myriad of drugs, never dealing with the abscesses that are buried beneath the surface. In this culture it is easier to medicate our children than it is to mediate what is wrong with them. Kip Kinkel, a 15-year-old student at Thurston High School in Springfield, Oregon, killed his parents and two classmates and wounded 22 other students in 1998. Kinkel was on Ritalin and Prozac, two common antidepressants. Eric Harris, one of the Columbine High School killers, was on the antidepressant drug Lavox. Thomas Soloman, a 15-year-old at Heritage High School in Conyers, Georgia, shot and wounded six classmates. Solomon was on Ritalin. There are many things wrong with children these days, and it doesn't seem like the medications are solving their problems.[1]

Of course, not every child who is on medication is going to become a serial killer. There are some children who need neurological help, and these drugs can be used in a responsible manner. However, I know that some of these kids don't need to be chemically kept under control. Instead, they need someone to help them learn how to forgive the adults in their lives who have hurt them.

When I was 16 I had a complete physical and emotional shutdown. A doctor was brought to the house because I was too ill—and too unwilling—to go to his office. While I was in the bathroom trying to take a bath before the doctor arrived, there was a moment when I thought I had died. The only thing that brought me around to the fact that I was still alive was when I realized, "I can't be dead because I still hurt so badly."

All the veins had collapsed in my legs, and I was completely out of control with my emotions. During that time of upheaval, I accompanied my mother to a funeral. That was a real mistake. My emotions were mixed up. Instead of crying when I was sad and laughing when I was happy, I would do the opposite. I found myself with an uncontrollable desire to laugh during the funeral. It was then that I realized just how messed up I was, yet I was helpless to do anything about it.

After a while I learned to cope, and eventually I returned to school. Nothing had changed in my life; all the root problems were still there. Some of the pressure had been relieved and I had simply learned to suppress my emotions and keep them under control. I wasn't crazy; I just needed some help. I finished my junior year of high school and went on to graduate on time.

My high school choir director encouraged me to apply to Moody Bible Institute. I did, and I was accepted. During my freshman year as a student at MBI, I attended my first of many Bill Gothard Seminars. It was subtitled "The Institute in Basic Youth Conflicts." It was there that for the first time I was introduced to the concept that our past has an influence on our ability to cope with our present circumstances.

I went to the meeting unaware that incidents in a person's history were often the source of the abscesses that lay just under the surface of their everyday life. By my late teens to early 20s, my coping mechanisms were well in place. Being in a different environment helped me suppress my problems with just occasional eruptions of passive and aggressive manifestations of my anger. However, my roommate at times observed some rather bizarre behavior. Whenever I would hear of an assault on a woman, for example, or any description of sexual perversion, I would start to hyperventilate. This was quite a nuisance, as I was relatively sane most of the time.

It was my forceful, will-not-take-no-for-an-answer room-mate who called a counselor at the Bill Gothard offices in a suburb of Chicago. My dear friend arranged for a driver to take us there. She accompanied me and literally forced me to talk to the counselor. I will be forever grateful to her for her actions.

Reaching Out

The initial appointment was scheduled to last a mere 30 minutes. I thought that would be more than enough time. Talking to a *man* about what had happened to me was the hardest thing I had ever done up to that point. As it turned out, my appointment stretched from 30 minutes to two hours. I don't remember the man's name, but I distinctly remember what he told me. I was desperate for help, and surprisingly I followed his instructions. I've been told that no one normally gets all the help they need in one session. However, I truly was sick and tired of the overwhelming anger that stormed inside me. I knew I had to have help; I could not go on living with the debilitating rage.

While counseling can be wonderful, it can also become part of the problem. When I hear someone say that he or she has been in counseling for a number of years, I surmise that the person either has a terrible counselor or is not following the counselor's advice. Being a victim offers a certain status these days. In fact, it has become a protected class. I get tired of hearing people blame inexcusable behavior on what happened years ago. When people identify themselves as victims, they get a lot of attention. Consequently, they will often hold on to the hurts because that is their strange source of comfort. Sometimes it is easier to live with the problem than to do the hard work of getting better.

While I was growing up, I had an uncle who hurt his hand. He went to the physician and the doctor worked his medical magic, then sent my uncle to a physical therapist to help get his hand back in working order. When my uncle discovered that the therapy required him to exercise the wounded appendage and that the effort produced a degree of pain, he refused to comply. The therapist explained to him that he would never regain full movement of his hand unless he did the work. That did not matter. He would not do the therapy. Eventually, my uncle's hand became paralyzed, the muscles atrophied, and it became a twisted, hideous claw. He had to wear it wrapped in a cloth to cover the useless extremity. If he had simply endured the initial pain, it is likely he would have had a usable hand. Instead, he took the easy way, but not the best way.

There are those who are paralyzed, crippled, ugly, and hideous because they refuse to do the hard work. What was the "work" the counselor told me to do? I had to forgive my offender. It was time for resolution.

Resolution

I recently heard someone say, "Unforgiveness is like drinking poison, expecting it to kill the other person." I fully understand that distorted way of thinking. I was operating under the impression that if I continued hating, my offender would be the one to suffer. Of course, I was wrong. The only person hurting under the weight of unforgiveness was me.

Knowing that I had to forgive in order to be free, I had a dilemma on my hands. Did I wait until the offender requested forgiveness? Or did I go ahead and extend it without his participation?

There are some who do not believe one should forgive without forgiveness being sought. They purport that God does not forgive unless we confess our sins and repent. However, human forgiveness and divine forgiveness are not the same.

Divine forgiveness is far different than human forgiveness. God's forgiveness has the power to *pardon* (1 John 1:9: "If we confess our sins, He is faithful and righteous to forgive us our sins, and to cleanse us from all unrighteousness"), to *forget* the sin (Psalm 103:12: "As far as the east is from the west, so far has He removed our transgressions from us"), and to *eradicate* the results of the sinful offense (John 3:16: "For God so loved the world, that He gave His only begotten Son, that whoever believes in Him should not perish, but have eternal life").

Human forgiveness, on the other hand, is simply forfeiting the right to revenge. The release is experienced only for the one who forgives. When we forgive, we are disconnecting ourselves from the offender. We are the one who is set free.

I feared forgiving because I thought I would be, in essence, saying that the unspeakable assault against me was excusable. That is in no way true. When I forgave the offender, I was unhooking myself from him. My forgiveness had no effect on his responsibility before God. He was still sin guilty, but I was finally free.

There were some simple steps (but not easy, I remind you!) that the counselor gave to me the day I visited his office. By following his scriptural advice consistently, I finally became free from the bondage of anger. I quote from my book *What Do I Want?*[2]

After I became a Christian, I became keenly aware that who and what I was supposed to be as a born-again believer was not who and what I was inside my heart and mind. I tried to live the Christian life in a moral, loving way. For the most part I experienced God's divine reconstruction work in my life. I desperately wanted to be that new creature in Christ with old things passing away and all things becoming new (2 Corinthians 5:17). There was great comfort in my heart as I recognized God's merciful work in my life. However, there was one area that seemed to hold me back. I hated the man who had harmed me. I hated him with a vengeance. So, even though I loved God and wanted His best for me, I was guilty of violating the heart of 1 John 4:20,21. "If someone says, 'I love God,' and hates his brother, he is a liar; for the one who does not love his brother whom he has seen, cannot love God whom he has not seen. And this commandment we have from Him, that the one who loves God should love his brother also."

Realizing that a Christian was supposed to love everyone and hate no one, I knew I had a problem. For a long time I would simply deny my thoughts of hatred toward the man. After talking to the counselor, I was challenged with the reoccurring thought that, "perhaps I should try BEING HONEST WITH GOD." So, whenever a thought of hatred and revenge came to my mind, instead of trying to push it back, I brought it out in the open. This was my first step toward opening the door of the prison I had been in for so long. I would EXPOSE MY THOUGHTS TO GOD in prayer. I would pray something like this: "Dear Lord, You see this vile, wicked thought that I am having. I know You see how much I want this person to die and go to hell. Lord, I give this thought, and all my thoughts, to You and ask You to forgive me and change my heart."

As I learned to be honest with God, I came to a very painful realization. All my life I had looked at the offense from the point of view as a child. My only perspective was one of innocence. I would say, "I was just a little child. I had done nothing wrong."

Of course, I was not responsible, in any way, for this particular sinful act. However, as long as I saw the situation as "I was the innocent child and he was the monster molester," there was no room for forgiveness. There was too big a chasm between the offender and me. It was only when I could admit that I too was a sinner, in the eyes of God, that I could see myself on the same level, needing the same undeserved grace, as the perpetrator.

So part of my exercise in honesty was recognizing my innate need for forgiveness. In Psalm 51:5 David states, "Behold, I was brought forth in iniquity, and in sin my mother conceived me." The "sin" condition was present, even though I was a child.

Along with *exposing my wicked thoughts*, I would take the second step to freedom. I would TURN MY THOUGHTS TO PRAYERS OF THANKSGIVING. I would pray, "Thank You, Lord, for this wicked thought because it has reminded me to pray and seek Your help. Thank You that You are my source of strength and You are not embarrassed by anything I could think or do."

Next, I would QUOTE SCRIPTURES on forgiveness and love, all the while concentrating on those passages to reaffirm the correctness of my prayers. The last part of my prayer was, by far, the most difficult. I would *pray that God would save the offender*, allow him to know God's grace, and take him to heaven. (I eventually discovered that it is very hard to keep hating someone when you are praying for them.)

Many times each day I would go through the same process. I understand the seventy times seven instruction that Jesus gave in Matthew 18:22. Though my emotions were far, far from sincere, I knew I had to discipline myself to follow through...because I was desperate to be free. Forgiveness was my only hope and I worked on it feverishly.

I started on this process to forgiveness out of an act of desperate obedience. Needing to be free from the torment of unforgiveness and anger, I obeyed the instructions of the counselor. I exercised my will to forgive. But, after a time, as my heart softened, my obedience turned from a soulish act of wanting to feel better, to a spiritual desire to honor God. After about six months, I woke up one morning and realized that the chains had fallen away. I was finally free! Was this the last time I had to struggle with this issue? I wish it was, but the same discipline that was needed in the first six months has been needed each time I've faced reminders and dealt with the residue effect of what was done to me. However, I gladly say, I am not a victim, I am a victor in Jesus Christ."

For years I have heard the saying, "It's not what has happened to you, but how you have reacted to it, and what you let your mind dwell on, that determines who you are." How true! The way we react to problems and situations in our lives has a profound impact on those around us. We have all known individuals who have gone through horribly difficult times in their lives. Some who are challenged in this way come out of it trusting in God and leaning on His understanding. They choose to love and depend on the wisdom of God, even though it doesn't make sense. And there are others who face trials and tests who become bitter and hateful. We are like tubes of toothpaste. When we get squeezed, what's inside comes out. Difficult circumstances simply reveal who we are.

Regardless of whether you have dealt victoriously with your challenge or failed miserably, God is able to use your suffering for your good and to His glory. As we obey the mandate of Romans 12:1-2, we will find a way to renew our thinking, and in doing so, we will enjoy the peace of God that passes understanding. That peace will guard our hearts and minds in Christ Jesus as we learn to think on whatever is true, honorable, right, pure, lovely, and of good repute (Philippians 4:8). With all of these wonderful virtues filling our minds, there will be less room for the anger and rage that seek to undo us.

4

Pride Goeth Before a Tantrum

"For everyone who exalts himself shall be humbled, and he who humbles himself shall be exalted."

—LUKE 14:11

If your source of irritation is a leaky faucet, then fix it or hire someone else to remedy the problem. If you are constantly angry because the phone rings during dinnertime, then get an answering machine or simply don't answer it. While there are many practical things we can do to eliminate a lot of the simple frustrations and sources of anger, dealing with some irritations requires more effort.

In one of our former neighborhoods, we had a cranky next-door neighbor. The day we moved in, they promptly erected a large privacy fence between our property and theirs. That was fine. However, it did alert us to a potential problem. It was not hard to figure out that these people did not relish having neighbors who had young children. (At the time, Nathan was eleven and Heidi was eight.)

The first time my son went into their yard to retrieve a stray basketball, we were told loudly and clearly that our children were not to trespass on their lawn for any reason. We made the children keenly aware of this restriction, and the kids made a valiant effort to comply.

There was a sense of tension whenever we talked or thought about our next-door neighbors. As our first Christmas on our new street approached, we began to see it as an opportunity to reach out to the unfriendly folks next door. As was our custom in our previous neighborhood, I made apple pies for each of my neighbors. (My record was 40 hand-peeled, hand-grated, home-made-crust pies. Please excuse my boasting, as well as my drool. But they were quite tasty, and I was confident our neighbors would enjoy a pie.) It was one of the highlights of the Christmas season for Nathan and Heidi as they looked forward to pre-senting the pies with a Christmas reminder that Jesus was the reason for the season.

When it came time to deliver the pie to our next-door neighbors, I dressed the children in their warmest coats and scarves. With pie in hand, they walked to our neighbors' house, careful to not cut across on the grass. They knocked on the front door. The man of the house came to answer it. He looked down at my adorable children, seeing their eager, shining faces beaming with Christmas spirit. He barked at them, "I don't want to buy anything!" And then he slammed the door.

The children were confused and hurt. Why had he refused their Christmas pie? Why had he been so mean to them? At first I was furious. Why had I even tried to reach out to someone so mean and nasty? After a moment of reflection, I realized I had two choices, but only one of them was the "godly" response.

Resisting my natural urge to ream out that grumpy old man, I swallowed my pride and called him on the phone. "Hello, Mr. _____," I said in the nicest voice I could fake. "I am so sorry I failed to call you before I sent the children next door. They just wanted to give you a Christmas pie; it isn't for sale. Would you allow them to come back with the pie?" He grunted something like, "Oh, I didn't know they were your kids."

I would like to say that was the end of our strained relationship with these people we barely knew. If I said that, it would not be true. The uneasy feelings continued to persist. However, this simple gesture gave us something to build on. There would be many opportunities to learn how to deal with our neighbors in the years that followed, and all of them involved me choosing peace over anger. My human pride got such a workout that my spirit should have looked like the buff, solid body of Evander Holyfield. Instead it seemed I faced each new challenge to humble myself as though I were a wet noodle. Any victories from battles previously fought seemed to have no effect. Each time I had to make the difficult decision to put pride aside and choose humility.

Dealing with the pride in my life reminds me of taking care of our dog. He's a sweet old thing named Bob. His breed is known as the Shiitzu. He gives us no trouble. He doesn't shed hair, chase cars, bite people, or run away when we let him go outside. Basically, Bob is content to eat, sleep, and give and receive love. We couldn't ask for a nicer pet. However, Bob has one persistent problem. He has ear infections. It's not his fault; it's just consistent with his breed. I suppose it is because of how the ears flop over and stay close to his head. They are a prime growing area for infection.

Because we know it is in his nature to have ear problems, we keep medication on hand at all times. There will never be a time, as long as Bob lives, that it will not be necessary to doctor his ears. We accept it as reality. We never give him ear drops with the assumption we have cured his problem. We understand it is an ongoing process.

The same is true when I am dealing with my tendency to be self-concerned and full of pride. It's in my nature, so to speak. My breed (human being) has a chronic, ongoing struggle with the infection of "pride." As long as I know I will have to battle it continuously, then I should not get discouraged when "pride" rears its ugly head.

Thankfully, I have found that God is very gracious to help me deal with the self-love that permeates my life. He does this by bringing people across my path who irritate me. My neighbors—getting back to them—were often used by God.

One situation really stands out in my mind. We came home from a weekend of ministry and were surprised to discover they had dug a large, deep ditch right beside our freshly-paved driveway. Actually, they had dug under the asphalt, severely undermining it. If left unremedied, it would take very little time before our driveway would begin to crumble. That was the last straw! I was ready to call the police for criminal trespassing. How dare they deliberately dig under the blacktop and destroy our property?

I gave my words full vent to everyone around me. I was pronouncing all kinds of accusations and assigning malicious motives to their actions. What they had done was inexcusable and beyond understanding. As I was ready to call the authorities, Steve said, "I'm going next door to talk with them." I thought, "Well, it's about time you stood up for this family! You'd better let them have it!"

Together we went next door. Steve walked up to the door. I stood silently behind him. (Anything I would have said would have only started a fight.) He knocked on the door and waited for someone to answer. When the woman of the house answered, Steve's words caught me totally by surprise. He quietly uttered, "Mrs._____, you must be very angry with us." Her face ignited and she said, "I sure am!"

Proverbs 25:8-9, warns us, "Do not go out hastily to argue your case; Otherwise, what will you do in the end, when your neighbor puts you to shame? Argue your case with your neighbor, and do not reveal the secret of another, lest he who hears it reproach you and the evil report about you not pass away."

Now, wait a minute. Who is angry at whom? The last time I looked, it was our driveway getting ready to cave in. It was our property line that had been compromised. Why was she mad at us?

Steve continued, "Tell me what is wrong." She began to explain how the previous owner of our house had built the driveway too close to their property line. Also, because the lot was on a slant, all the water drained from our yard, running down the driveway and washing out all the grass in their backyard. They took matters into their own hands and dug up our driveway, creating a drainage ditch for runoff water.

None of the water problems had been caused by us. The disagreement had been with the previous owner of our house, yet we were the ones left to deal with irritated neighbors. Steve responded, "Let me see if I can remedy this problem. With your permission, I will fill in the ditch you dug with concrete so our drive will not wash away. And also, if it's agreeable with you, I will dig the ditch on down the property line past your backyard so as not to disturb your soil. I will pour that trench with concrete as well, if that's all right with you."

The whole time Steve was talking I was speechless. Why was he being so nice to these hateful people? The truth be told, I was too angry and too blind to see that Steve was not only digging a ditch for our neighbor, but he was also building a bridge to them. That day, by the loving, humble, Christlike manner with which Steve treated our neighbor, he tactfully avoided a feud that could have likely ended up in a courtroom.

Instead of being our enemies, those people began to speak to us when we went into our yard. They were never what you could call overly friendly, but they were no longer hostile. Whenever the woman needed a ladder, or help of any kind, she always came and asked for Steve. Eleven years later, the morning we were packing to leave to move to our present residence, the lady came over and sat and had coffee with us. She seemed really sorry to see us move.

What had Steve done? He put pride aside and humbled himself. He regarded our neighbors as more important than our driveway. He knew that Jesus died out of love for those people who lived next door to us. Regardless of how they acted, He wanted us to love them, too. I'm grateful that Steve lived the life of Jesus in front of them. It took me longer to come around to it, but eventually even my old cold heart got it right.

When I pray and ask God to make me more like Jesus, I am asking for opportunities to be humbled and to conduct myself in a gentle way toward those who would seek to hurt me. This is not the American way of thinking, but it is the way of Christ. As far as I know, there is only one place in the Scriptures where

Jesus offers a description of himself. In Matthew 11:29, He says, "…for I am gentle and humble in heart."

Jesus also said in Luke 14:11, "For everyone who exalts himself shall be humbled, and he who humbles himself shall be exalted." I could see it in the face of this neighbor. She exalted Steve that day to the status of a truly "big man." It is obvious I was not as blessed or as meek.

I've learned that if I do not humble myself, God keeps giving me opportunities (in other words, problems) to get it right. As if the driveway problem was not a good enough lesson, consider the time we were vandalized during one of our concert trips. Steve and I stayed in a very nice hotel when we were singing in Columbus, Ohio. Since the city is just seven or eight hours from where we live, we toyed with the idea of driving all night to get home instead of spending the night in Ohio. However, I had not been feeling well the evening before, so we opted to stay in the hotel, get up early the next morning, and drive home to Tennessee.

The next day we got up to leave at 5:30 A.M. When Steve went out to put the luggage in the van, he discovered that the back side window had been crushed in. After looking around the parking lot, we saw another car that had suffered a similar fate.

Steve looked inside the van to see what was missing. Thankfully, he didn't notice anything was gone. We went into the hotel to inform the people at the desk of what had happened and asked them to call the police.

We stayed around for about an hour and no police officer showed up. Thinking it was only a broken window and just a matter for the insurance company, we decided to go ahead and leave Columbus. It wasn't until about six hours later, when we decided to stop at an antique store, that I discovered my purse had been lifted from the van. I never leave my purse in a vehicle, and never in the back of the van. However, the night before, feeling sick, I had gone back to lie down on the bench. It was then that I had left my purse there.

Well, when we discovered my purse missing, everything changed. This criminal had our checkbook, my driver's license, our credit cards, my Social Security card, every form of identification possible. The thief had been in possession of this information for many hours without our knowledge. As soon as I could pull my mind together, I remembered that I was supposed to pray for my enemy (Matthew 5:44). So I did. I prayed, "Dear Lord, whoever broke out the window in our van and stole my purse, please squish him like a bug!" I knew very well that was not the intent of that verse, but at the time that was all I could come up with. We hurried to get home and started calling the credit card people as soon as we walked in the door.

I suppose criminals know what they are doing. By stealing on a Friday night and not being discovered until Saturday morning, they have more opportunity to spend the stolen money, and it takes much more time and effort to put a stop on the credit cards. Steve and I were on two different phone lines for four hours calling credit card companies. Sometimes we would be placed on hold for as long as half an hour. We were involved in this tedious process all afternoon. Many hours later it occurred to us that we had not called our bank to stop payment on checks and to cancel the ATM card.

In a complete panic, I called the bank and was put on hold for another half hour. Finally, a woman came on the telephone line. After telling her I had been robbed, I asked her to please stop payment on a book of checks and to cancel my ATM card.

She pulled up my name and announced in an irritated tone of voice, "You don't have an ATM card."

Of course I knew I had one, so I replied, "I do have a card; I just don't ever use it. Perhaps it's not activated." She answered gruffly, "No, you don't. You might have a credit card, but you don't have an ATM card." She continued to yell at me, saying I was wrong. It was at that time I knew I had a choice to make. I thought about the scriptures that speak of "humbling yourself" and "putting on humility." At the time I didn't *feel* humble. I felt tired, beaten down, and abused, but I certainly didn't feel the least bit humble.

However, in the midst of my tormented mind, I realized a truth I had overlooked all my life. God didn't say, "Be humble." He said, "Humble yourself." At that moment I chose to physically humble myself. I relaxed my shoulders, lowered my voice, and meekly said, "Yes, ma'am."

I realized as I was doing this spiritual act of obedience that I could have taken a different route. In my flesh, I wanted to threaten her by asking for her name. I was tempted to roughly tell her how many accounts we had with that particular banking chain. I could have said, "I will have your job for talking to me like that. I want to talk to your supervisor." I could have, and perhaps I would have been justified in doing so. But you see, I didn't have all the authority here. I needed her to do a job for me. If I pulled rank on her, she didn't have to help me.

As I sat at the kitchen table with the phone to my ear and my jaw in my hand, I thought of a time when I exercised my own authority and the weapon of my tongue and it got me into the proverbial pickle. Steve and I were doing some remodeling inside our house. We had a new electric box installed that offered more amps. The inspector was scheduled to come one morning, but he didn't show up at all that day. I was ticked off, having spent the entire day waiting for him. When he arrived the following day, I told him how much I didn't appreciate being kept waiting. I said something along the lines of, "Look, buddy, you are a government worker. You work for me!" Isn't it amazing that our electrical job didn't pass inspection? I then got to wait for him to come on another day!

I knew I could vent my anger on the lady at the bank, but, thankfully, this particular time I took the path of humility. I quietly asked her about stopping payment on the missing checkbook. She yelled back at me, "That was the next thing I was going to get to." My response: "Yes, ma'am."

After going through all of that she then told me that the "stop payment" on the checks would not take effect until Tuesday morning. It would take a full working business day to process all the paperwork. Oh, no! The thief had from Saturday morning until Tuesday morning to write checks. I was sick again. However, I humbly said, "Yes, ma'am." Then, to my amazement and surprise, something remarkable happened that I will never forget. Her tone of voice completely changed. She said, "You've had a hard day, haven't you?" My response was a quiet, "Yes, ma'am." To my astonishment she began consoling me. She said, "Look, it's going to be all right. If the bank or a store cashes your checks without looking at your license and seeing that the person is not you, you won't have to pay. It's going to be all right."

Everything changed when I chose to "humble myself" and kept "humbling myself" even in the face of continuing abuse. All my life I thought God expected me to "be humble." That was frustrating for me because I'm a take-charge person who is not afraid of confrontation. Despite whatever my family may think,

I don't actually enjoy a fight, but I won't run from one either. It is hard for me to act meek and mild. But it was a revelation to realize that even though it does not come naturally to me, I can choose to humble myself.

Choosing humility that day stopped anger in its tracks. Anger and humility cannot coexist. They are opposites. The biggest help was knowing that I could trust God and act as though everything really does come through the filter of His love. That understanding gave me the peace of mind to choose humility. As a result, I was able to stop fighting for my own way.

When we cease living as though we are the one in charge of all aspects of our lives and allow God to be in control, only then can we give the things that interfere with our plans—a long line at the grocery store, a fender-bender in the parking lot, a canceled airplane flight—over to our heavenly Father.

Relinquishing control to God sets us free from the stress and the strain of life. We get up in the morning and pray, "Dear Lord, I give You this day. I want to follow You and do what You want me to do." That may be how we start, but too many times we end the day by praying, "Dear Lord, it's been a horrible day. Nothing has gone right. I didn't accomplish any of the things I wanted to do. Please, don't let tomorrow be like today."

Have we just insulted God? On one hand, we give Him full reign of our day; on the other hand, we complain that He really messed up. The truth is, the day's struggles that we might have resented could very well have been precisely what He planned in order to continue forming us into His image.

5

Anger: The Game Nobody Wins!

"And do not be conformed to this world, but be transformed by the renewing of your mind, that you may prove what the will of God is, that which is good and acceptable and perfect."

—Romans 12:2

The well-known American humorist Will Rogers once said, "People who fly into a rage always make a bad landing." I have skidded down the runway of rage a time or two in my lifetime. Anger seems to take on a power of its own.

Like many others, I have attributed my tendency toward openly expressed anger as something just a bit out of my control. There have been times when I blamed my rude outbursts on my heritage. For years I thought it was my great-grandfather's fault that I was so angry. He's the one who contributed my German ancestry. I would say, "Well, I'm sorry I was so unkind, but it's just that hot-blooded German coming out in me." It wasn't till years later that I learned he wasn't a German, he just lived in Germany. So I had to discover a new ethnic heritage to blame.

I'm not the only one who has done this. I've heard people blame their Irish, Italian, or Hispanic bloodlines. It's as though some unsuspecting ancestor from generations past is the one who "made them do it."

Some folks blame their immediate family for their unseemly and hateful behavior. One might say, "My father was an alcoholic, and so now I can't help it that I'm a rage-aholic." Others may claim, "All the women in my family are hot-tempered. That's just who we are." And some even blame it on the color of their hair! Since our son has red hair and loves to hunt, we have always jokingly accused him that he was happiest when he was killing something.

There is some validity to the argument that we learn to be who we live with. However, our heavenly Father seeks to replace those fleshly examples with His influence. To do so He might lead us to Romans 12:1-2, where we find His spiritual remedy for our natural tendency toward ungodly behavior. First, we offer our lives as living sacrifices to God. Then we allow His conforming and transforming work to take place through the renewing of our minds by saturating our lives with the Word of God and His presence. While it is true that our families do influence us, we are supposed to choose to emulate our "new family," with God as our Father.

In recent years, with medical research at the forefront, it has become more common to blame our problems with temper on a physical or a chemical imbalance in our bodies. "My son can't help his outrageous behavior because he suffers from ADD (Attention Deficit Disorder), or ADHD (Attention Deficit Hyperactive Disorder), or even ODD (Obstinate Defiance Disorder)," people reason. There are a few children and adults who actually do suffer from severe neurological disorders that require them to be involved with ongoing medical treatment. While that might explain some of the undesirable behavior problems, the truth is that many of us suffer from what is more commonly referred to as MAD (I-don't-like-it-when-I-don't-get-my-way-and-you're-going-to-pay disorder).

Some blame their problem with anger on the people in their lives, others impugn the circumstances of their childhood. "I was abused as a child. I was rejected from the womb. No one picked me for 'Red Rover, Red Rover, Let _____ Come Over.' I never heard my name called out for the softball lineup." These are hurts that often follow us into our adult years. We can feel rejected and angry, but there comes a time when we must forgive and let God heal the wounded places in our lives. I am so grateful that God does not leave us without a balm of healing. Others may have rejected us and passed over us as though we were nothing. But if we know Christ, we can no longer claim this slight. Romans 5:6-8 reassures us that, "For while we were still helpless, at the right time Christ died for the ungodly. For one will hardly die for a righteous man; though perhaps for the good man someone would dare even to die. BUT GOD DEMONSTRATES HIS OWN LOVE TOWARD US, IN THAT WHILE WE WERE YET SINNERS, CHRIST DIED FOR US" (all caps mine).

Blaming an individual, a group of people, a physical problem, or circumstances from our past for our uncontrolled, destructive outbursts of anger is not going to help. We will constantly face the challenge of whether we are going to win the anger game or whether we are going to be beaten up again. I know one thing: If I fail to deal rightly with my anger, I will always have other opportunities to try to get it right, because one thing is for sure—God loved me and accepted me just the way I was when I first came to Him. Thankfully, He loves me too much to leave me that way.

In recent years, He provided a unique "opportunity" that allowed me to learn a valuable lesson about dealing with ongoing anger. It involved another move to a new home. What should have been an exciting and fun time turned into a complicated situation.

We signed the contract to buy our house with the stipulation that the seller would leave behind all the curtains. We made this same concession in the house we sold and considered it to be a reasonable request. Everyone signed the contracts and the closing date was set.

The day we moved into our house was a typical day of busy confusion. Everything was a beehive of activity. Several friends had come to help, along with family members and some hired help for the day. It wasn't until near the end of the evening, as things began to settle down, that I realized there was something different about our new house. It took me a little time to figure it out, and then it sank in. There were no curtains in the bedrooms, living room, or dining room. The seller had simply changed her mind and taken the curtains with her. This might seem insignificant in the face of all the bad that happens in the world, but in my little hemisphere this was an outrage.

We had given the woman who was selling the house her asking price. Since she was a widow and in poor health, we didn't have the heart to talk her off the amount she wanted. We didn't want to take advantage of her. Little did we know, we were the ones who needed to run for cover.

I was infuriated with everyone involved in the whole process, including Steve, since he thought I was overreacting. Beyond all logical reasoning, the real estate agent sided with the seller and refused to help us retrieve "our" curtains, even though the agent knew what her client had done was illegal.

Day after day, the injustice of it all ate away at me. We called a lawyer and threatened to sue everyone involved. At this point the monetary value of the curtains didn't matter. It would cost more to sue than to go buy more window treatments. However, the anger factor made the money matter irrelevant. I was not going to stand by and let them take advantage of me. I would fight for my rights (my curtains) to the bitter end.

Steve was not as emotionally invested in this situation. He thought I was mad over curtains. But the anger had taken on a life of its own. I was enraged over being robbed and lied to.

And I *was* being robbed. The joy of making the house my home dwindled more and more every time I walked into a room. All I saw were empty windows. I got into a state of mind where I couldn't relax. Every time I would go for a walk or mow the grass, I would rehearse what I would say to each offender involved.

Finally, after twisting in the wind for weeks with my gut in a wad, my son Nathan shared some words of wisdom. I was spouting off, telling everyone what I thought about the real estate agent's ridiculous offer to settle for $300 in lieu of the curtains. (Any woman realizes just how little money $300 is when you have to dress 12 windows.) As I was delivering my verbal tirade, Nathan said, "Mom, in a war, no one wins. They just agree to stop fighting."

I definitely had not won the "War of the Curtains," but as I continued the fray I was losing much more than window treatments. I was losing the pleasure of being with my family. I was not enjoying the beautiful spring weather and the lovely flowers. The fight was sucking the life out of me and thus out of my relationship with God. I knew I had allowed my anger to go way over the line. Many nights I had gone to bed with the enemy of my soul, allowing the sun to go down and still being angry. The devil had a foothold in my life, and it had little to do with curtains.

In agreement with Nathan's advice, I took the inadequate amount of cash, went to J.C. Penney's, and bought $300 worth of lacy curtains. They were not the expensive, custom-made treatments we were suppose to receive with the house. But as the days went by, I came to realize I liked the lighter, less formal look. Now, four years later, the same curtains hang at the windows, and I actually prefer them. They are a reminder to not let anger come and live with me again. What started out as someone else's sin (stealing "my" curtains) had been overshadowed by my own.

There were times during the "window wars" that I felt overtaken. If allowed, anger can have that kind of power. And, as if it were not bad enough that sources attack from outside my heart, there was another time much earlier in my life that my inner self became my own worst enemy. In this case, I unwittingly used someone else's vengeful outburst of angry words to plot my own demise.

In the past I used weight to mask my self-loathing. After the assault as a child which I mentioned in a previous chapter, I needed to develop some ways to fight the anger that engulfed me. With no other ways—as far as I knew—to make me feel better, I began to eat. Consequently, I started to gain weight. There were many around me more than willing to point out the fact that I had a growing poundage problem. As a result of my larger size, I became a target for cruel and mean comments about my appearance. Eventually, my weight became the focus rather than the real problem, which was my unresolved anger and bitterness. And that's exactly the way I wanted it.

My battle against myself started the day a neighbor lady came to visit with my mother. I was around 10 years old at the time, and I was not a part of their conversation. However, I walked into the room as they were talking. It was then that the woman looked up at me in what I perceived as disgust and said, "She's a sow!"

For all you non-farm folk, a sow is an old female hog. It didn't go unnoticed that she didn't call me one of the cute, pink, little curly-tailed piglets. No, she called me an old, flabby, ugly hog! Unfortunately, I never forgot that comment. Those words of critique and criticism rang in my ears. It was a matter of years before I realized a shocking truth. The woman was a relative of the man who raped me. I can only surmise that she and Mom were discussing the incident when I walked in. The woman never came to our house again after that day. Perhaps she was expressing her anger over the situation by attacking me and calling me names. I'm sure she was hurt and understandably angry. I assumed she chose to direct her outrage on someone else. It just happened to be me.

After the comment by our neighbor, I began to see myself the way I thought others saw me. Being the brunt of cruel comments and jokes about my weight, I simply gave up.

I recall the day when everything changed for the worse. I was in the sixth grade, and my elementary school cafeteria was serving spaghetti and meatballs for lunch. As I sat and ate my meal, I started thinking about my weight and my unattractive appearance. By the way, I weighed 125 pounds. At 12 years old I was heavier than I should have been, but I was not the gigantic monster I thought I was.

That day, I went back for a second helping of spaghetti, and then a third. The decision to give in to destructive eating habits set the stage for much misery and pain that followed. Today as I reflect back on the neighbor lady's comment, I see that it was both mean-spirited and unjustified. However, through the process of forgiveness, I no longer willfully take the sharp spear of her cutting words and thrust them into my own heart. And I have pardoned her for her angry attack.

Why do we hurt ourselves long after the offender has left? Why is it that we turn anger inward and continue to inflict throbbing pain? Why do we overeat, hoping it will make us feel better when it only leaves us fat? Why do we overspend, buying things we don't need (and sometimes don't even take out of the box), seeking to numb the pain? I know one woman who was disappointed with her life as a stay-at-home mom. She thought if she had a job, she would feel important and accomplished. Being the overachieving, ambitious woman she is, she took on a job working 60 hours a week for a demanding employer. Did it fix her problem of low self-worth? No, it just left her tired and more angry than ever.

Many of us struggle with the anger war that rages in us. Words from the past scream accusations of worthlessness. And as I did, we too often use them to whip ourselves. The messages from our younger years remind us of our sinful indulgences, and we come away thrusting the sword deeper and deeper into our bleeding wounds.

Because of the healing work of Christ in my life, I can now look back at the hurtful words of that woman from long ago and put them where they belong. I am no longer that young, chubby girl. Instead, I have resources through my relationship with God and the power of His Word to help me close those wounds of the past.

Who wins the anger wars? When Steve was a little boy someone asked him, "When you and your sister fight, who wins?" He answered, "Daddy!" In order for my heavenly Father to come out on top, I know I must always remember that the real enemy is not visible. He is not the curtain-snatching seller I encountered when we moved, nor is he the unscrupulous real estate agent. He is not the nasty woman, nor her degrading comments. The real enemy is not even the self-condemning spears I throw at myself. Instead, he is exposed in Ephesians 6:12: "For our struggle is not against flesh and blood, but against the rulers, against the powers, against the world forces of this darkness, against the spiritual forces of wickedness in the heavenly places." To know this truth is the key to winning the war against anger.

6

God Thought Cain Was Able

"He who is slow to anger is better than the mighty, and he who rules his spirit [attitude] than he who captures a city."

—PROVERBS 16:32

One of my favorite television shows is the one featuring Judge Judy. (Should I have admitted that? Well, it's too late now!) The idea behind the show involves the retired Judge (Judy Sheindlin) who adjudicates cases that would normally have been tried in a civil court. However, the litigants have agreed to have their cases heard and tried in an entertainment/court-like setting.

No matter what I'm doing, I stop when it's time for her show. I sit down and watch her performance. Perhaps I am intrigued with her demeanor because she's mean and actually gets paid the "big bucks" to act that way. I want her job! You see, I do the same work that she does. I judge people harshly, give unsolicited opinions, am just as cantankerous as she is, but unfortunately, I don't get paid a salary.

In a recent show the plaintiff (the person who's mad) was suing the defendant (her sister) for $150. It seemed the one sister had gotten her sibling involved in a money-making scheme that didn't pan out, and the angry sister had lost her money. The judge ruled in favor of the plaintiff, and she was returned her investment. At the end of the show, when they interviewed the parties involved, they asked the woman suing if she could be reconciled to her sister. Her angry answer was an emphatic, "No!" By all indications, the relationship between the two had been permanently severed over a mere $150. What a pity that the return of the money had not tempered the angry feelings of one sister toward another. I got the impression that it wasn't the loss of money that was the issue.

Anger has been a problem as long as there have been people. In Genesis chapter 4 we read about Cain and his brother, Abel. When God rejected the offering of Cain—because it was not done in accordance with God's instructions—Cain became jealous of the acceptable sacrifice made by his brother. As a result, Cain became very angry. In Genesis 4:6-7 we read, "Then the LORD said to Cain, 'Why are you angry? And why has your countenance fallen? If you do well, will not your countenance be lifted up? And if you do not do well, sin is crouching at the door; and its desire is for you, but you must master it.'"

The word for anger in the Hebrew was the word *charah*, which means "to burn or glow with rage; to be incensed." This derivative appears 139 times in the Old Testament. It refers to the fire or the heat of anger just after it is ignited. This is a dangerous form of fury. It is in reference to "in the heat of the moment, or the heat of anger."

In verse 6 when God questions Cain, He asks him "why" he looked so mad. God then gives him the immediate remedy for this burning hostility. God says, "If you do well, will not your countenance be lifted up?" The Hebrew word for "well" is *yatab*, which indicates a correlation between things being right between God and the person. This word is used 105 times in the Old Testament referring to the connection between God and man. The profound implication in this truth is that the vertical relationship has a direct influence on the horizontal. Try as we may, we will not be able to skirt this divine arrangement!

After God instructed Cain concerning the real problem (his relationship between God and man), He then gave a stern warning to Cain: "...sin is crouching at the door; and its desire is for you, but you must master it." God wanted this young man to master it, to control it. Did God think Cain was *able*? Of course He did. Otherwise, He would not have asked him to take charge of his attitude. It was very good advice. Unfortunately, Cain did not heed it. Instead, he immediately lured Abel into a field and killed him. Nothing has been the same since that angry, murderous action. People have continued through the generations to allow anger to rule over them, ignoring the fact that the problem is really between them and God.

When we live in a state of hidden, seething anger, eventually something happens to bring it out. Anger may be revealed when your child spills grape juice on your white suit, or when you trip over the dog and go sprawling. Or perhaps anger is revealed when your spouse asks you to get him the ketchup, or when the baby messes his diaper—again. The "trigger" may not have been the negligent or childish act or accident, but the unsettled, seething anger from days, months, years, even a childhood ago, that reflects a breach in the relationship between you and God.

Archibald Hart expands the idea of mastering anger in his book, *Feeling Free:*

> The need to differentiate between anger (the feeling) and hostility/aggression (the behavior arising out of the feeling) is even more important when we turn to understanding the New Testament's approach to the problem of anger. The Apostle Paul presents us with what at first seems to be an impossible paradox: "Be ye angry, and sin not; let not the sun go down upon your wrath" (Ephesians 4:26). How can one be angry and sin not? The New English Bible translation makes a little clearer what the Apostle Paul was saying and provides us with a very up-to-date understanding not only of the nature of anger but also of its solution: "If you are angry, do not let anger lead you into sin; do not let the sunset find you still nursing it…" My understanding of what Paul is saying here is that it is not the anger itself (as feeling) that is wrong, but the anger has the potential for leading you into sin. The point is that it is the translation or conversion of anger feelings into aggressive and hostile acts that leads us into sin. To feel anger, to tell someone that you feel angry, and to talk about your anger are both healthy and necessary. As long as you recognize the anger as your own and avoid hurting back the object of your anger, you are keeping it as a feeling—and all feelings are legitimate! What you do with your feeling may not be [legitimate], and this is where you can fall into sin![1]

Dealing with anger is a part of the human plight. In Ephesians 4:26, which was just referenced, we are told that we *can* be angry, but we are not supposed to sin. The Greek word used in Ephesians 4 for anger is the word *paraorgismos*, which indicates the everyday annoyances of life. The word means irritations and exasperations. These are low-level aggravations, and we must take steps to keep the angry feelings appropriately on the controlled side of the line.

Life is filled with bothersome, infuriating situations and circumstances. It takes a person who is not truly plugged in all the way to reality to come through this life never angry or aggravated. It is my estimation that if our anger was charted on a graph that ranges from 1 to 10 (1 = at peace and not angry at all, and 10 = murderous rage), most people live life at an "8," just below the boiling point.

It seems that nearly all the women I talk to about this issue of anger inform me that they live constantly in the 5-9 range. To illustrate, consider two women in Alabaster, Alabama. On November 10, 1999, both were coming home from work when, it is assumed, one of them cut the other one off in busy traffic. Whatever the perceived driving infraction, the anger flared (*charah!*) and a pursuit of four to five miles began. Exchanging insults and obscene gestures, their tempers continued to burn. The situation escalated when, tragically, both women got off the interstate at the same exit. Evidently the woman in the lead car stopped and got out of her vehicle, flailing her arms and shouting obscenities. It was reported that the woman sitting in the car behind her had two items in her hands. In one hand she held a cell phone, in the other hand a .38-caliber handgun. Which one would she use?

It was reported that the woman outside her vehicle violently cursed at the lady behind the wheel, then abruptly spit in her face. The disrespected woman sitting behind the steering wheel suddenly answered back with a bullet in the face of the irate stranger.

How could this horrible incident have possibly happened? Two decent, hardworking women, one is now dead, the other presumably on her way to facing murder charges. It is said that the one who fired the gun was only five minutes away from her house.

Oh, how tragic for everyone! And it is especially horrifying to hear that the woman who shot her offender had the two items in her hands. With a cell phone, she could have called for help. She could have reached outside of her own inability to deal with the situation and asked for assistance. However, instead of making a call, she decided to make a kill. Call or kill? We all face this kind of choice daily. We can reach out and ask for help, or we can do what comes naturally and "shoot" those around us with venomous words of hatred that boil inside of us.

In light of that Alabama example of uncontrolled rage, I am thankful for those times when I "rule over anger" instead of letting it control me. Those times when I do it right always leave a lasting impression in my mind, perhaps because they are not as frequent as I wish they were. Just as God thought Cain was "able" to rule over his anger, He thinks I am able also. And when I allow His strength to be perfected in my weakness (2 Corinthians 12:9), it always turns out better for all concerned.

I remember one such time recently when I called on God for help to rule over my anger instead of "shooting off my mouth." My daughter, Heidi, and her soon-to-be husband came for a visit one weekend. They wanted to take me out to a nice restaurant for lunch. Steve was out of town, so it was just going to be the three of us.

We went to downtown Nashville and immediately started looking for a parking spot. We pulled into Central Parking and found a spot along the side, space 24. We walked out of the lot the way we had driven in, put our six dollars in the slot for space 24, and went in to the restaurant to enjoy a nice meal. We had plans for the rest of the afternoon, so we didn't linger long over lunch. Within an hour we came back to the parking lot. When we got to space 24, we were shocked to find it empty. I immediately thought someone had stolen my minivan. But it wasn't long until we learned it had been towed away. Dumbfounded, we walked toward a young man working at the opposite end of the lot. I told him that our vehicle had been towed away by mistake. It was then that I learned there were two parking lots that merged into one another. There were no signs posted to say where one parking lot ended and the other began. An unsuspecting person could come in one end and pay and be towed out the other end, just as had happened to us that day.

There was something about the young man in charge that didn't seem right. I immediately feared that I was a victim of a scam. Our conflict only worsened when he chose to demean me personally by calling me "sweetie." That verbal slight was not at all appreciated, nor did it go unchallenged. I said in a very firm voice, "Don't call me 'sweetie.' I'm old enough to be your mother, *son*!" I had to repeat that same statement each time he lapsed into calling me "sweetie." It was then that I demanded a police officer come and mediate the situation. I feared that I was dealing with a criminal element.

The young man said he had called the police, yet too much time had elapsed and no police officer had shown up. This made me even more suspicious. I sent Heidi and her fiancé to call the police. As I waited for them to arrive, I prayed, "Dear God, send me a person who will fight for me."

I was willing to submit to the police, even if it meant paying $65 for the towing of my car. But I would not pay it until someone was arbitrating the situation who was truly an authority figure. Eventually, after we called a couple of times, a patrolman came. I explained my problem to him and expressed my fear that I was being taken advantage of. The policeman asked the young man to get his boss on the phone. As he had done previously with us, the kid placed the call to his boss, but the truth be known, he knew the office was closed on a Saturday afternoon.

Actually, I think the parking lot attendant thought if he kept us waiting, we would grow impatient, pay the tow fee, and leave him alone. He didn't have any idea what a determined person I can be. I was going to stay if I had to sleep on the sidewalk. He was messing with the wrong "sweetie"!

I informed the policeman that I suspected the telephone number the young man was calling was bogus. The policeman growled at the kid, "Get me your boss…*now*!" Without hesitation, the kid called his supervisor's cell phone, and he answered immediately. The patrolman mediated between the manager of the lot and me. The owner offered to split the cost of the tow and agreed to put up signs to show where the two lots divided.

Was I wrong for not humbling myself and saying, "Yes, sir" to the parking attendant that day? Was I wrong to refuse to pay the tow until I found a police officer to help me? In each case, no. I submitted to the one in authority. The kid was not the one in command, the policeman was. I believe in that case I was angry, but I did not sin. I humbled myself to the policeman, even though I did not obey the parking attendant.

By the way, Heidi—bless her heart—was deeply concerned that her future groom was going to get a negative impression of his mother-in-law-to-be. Actually, I'm glad to report he was quite impressed with how I handled the situation. He also enjoyed the ride in the patrolman's car when the officer gave us a lift to the towing company to rescue my van.

When I was standing on the sidewalk, my heart was crying out for a mediator. I knew I had a great need, but I was helpless to meet it. Responding rightly to a situation that produces anger is not easy, but we have help available…if we call out. God only requires of us what Micah 6:8 says: "…to do justice, to love kindness, and to walk humbly with your God…."

Going to any source other than our heavenly Father for the assistance required to be victorious in our anger will always leave us shortchanged. There is a picture of how the world leaves us wanting when it comes to getting the help we need. It comes from my mother, who was a wealth of much knowledge and wisdom. Throughout my childhood her stories peppered my heart and mind. I recall her telling me about a very poor family that lived in her Appalachian region of West Virginia. Every family was poor in this hardworking community, but some were poorer than others. Although there was little or no money, the families were decent people who were caught in situations beyond their control. Unemployment was high, the Depression had hit, and it was devastating. Many of the sons had left their homes to fight in the Big War. Of those who survived, some came back only to fight poverty and destitution.

My Grandma Eckard was a sweet, generous woman, and her giving started at home. My mother recalled the morning that Grandma had only one egg to feed her family of eight. She made her "poor man's gravy," which was a white flour concoction made with water. Then she happily announced to the family that everyone could have some egg because she had mixed it into the gravy.

Miss Omie, as my sweet Grandma Eckard was known, was often called upon to go beyond her home and render service to her community. She did so without reservation. Whenever a neighbor baby was born or someone was sick or dying, Miss Omie could be found exercising her loving skills. She was an excellent midwife, nurse, and undertaker. Whatever needed to be done, she was there to help.

One day Miss Omie was called to one of the poorest families in the area. Mrs. Wilson was sick, and it was feared she was dying. As Miss Omie entered the house, she said she could literally smell death in the air. The house was filled with hungry, dirty, neglected children. The family was so destitute that the kids had what appeared to be the mange. There were large sections of their heads where hair could not grow either from the filth or malnutrition, or both. Miss Omie observed a hard crust of moldy bread sitting by the bedside of the dying mother. One of the children walked over to the nightstand, picked up the crust of bread, gnawed it, and then put it back. The scene was both heartbreaking and totally unacceptable.

Miss Omie returned to her home and told her husband, my grandfather Clarence, the situation. She said, "I know we are all poor and hungry, but we have neighbors who are starving to death right under our noses. We can't let this happen."

Grandpa Clarence promptly harnessed up the horses to the buckboard wagon and began going from house to house. My mother went along with him. Everyone gave, even from their own poverty. Families went into their root cellars and gave items such as vegetables, dried fruits, and canned meat. They went to their smokehouses and gave food reserved for their own tables to help these starving neighbors.

My mother remembered going with her dad to the one house where they believed they would receive the most help. The family that resided there had the nicest house in the community. They were the most educated, and they always seemed to have plenty to eat. When the need was explained to them, they reluctantly went into their attic and brought down some old purses for the starving family.

As Grandpa and my mother drove away, they were a little surprised at the offering of this well-to-do family. Then the thought occurred to Mom, "Perhaps there is money in the purses." Eagerly, she opened each one and as she did, she discovered each was empty. What were they thinking? My mother facetiously said, "Well, now the starving family can put all their money in the purses." The emptiness of the gift was overwhelming.

My mother has since gone home to be with the Lord, but the lesson of the "empty purses" remains. We come into the world starving to death, filthy with sin and despair. Ephesians 2:1,2,4-6 says:

> And you were dead in your trespasses and sins, in which you formerly walked according to the course of this world, according to the prince of the power of the air, of the spirit that is now working in the sons of disobedience…. But God, being rich in mercy, because of His great love with which He loved us, even when we were dead in our transgressions, made us alive together with Christ (by grace you have been saved), and raised us up with Him, seated us with Him in the heavenly places, in Christ Jesus.

We are ravaged with anger, bitterness, and unforgiveness. When we go to places like the self-help books and the encounter groups, all they can offer us is "empty purses." Regardless of their good intentions, the world has little—if any—assistance to offer in our quest to manage anger. Only God can help us "rule over" our spirits. And the best news is, He thinks we're able!

7

Is Honesty Always the Best Policy?

"A fool always loses his temper, but a wise man holds it back."

—PROVERBS 29:11

Anger can be such an undercurrent in our lives and such a normal part of our days that we come to believe it is not actually wrong. Our demeanor can be a temperament influenced by anger, and yet we call it something different. For example, we might refer to ourselves as "opinionated" or "high spirited," when in fact we are simply touchy and acrimonious. Taking a candid look at what makes us behave the way we do is not always pleasant. For instance, one day I was talking to a woman who said, "I feel like I have to be honest with my husband. When I think he's wrong and acting like an idiot, I need to tell him what I think." Oh, boy! I imagine that guy has a fun life.

Since I've had brutal honesty dished out to me, let me tell you—it doesn't taste that great! One night after a concert Steve and I were going to drive back to our lodging near the airport, a trip of about four hours. Knowing we would arrive very late to our room, I decided to remove my makeup and change into my travel uniform of blue jeans and sweatshirt before our drive. On our way out of town we stopped by a quick food spot to get something to eat. As I was standing at the counter a lady approached and explained that she and her husband had attended our concert that same evening. She gave words of appreciation for our ministry and then said something quite strange. "This evening I was sitting in the balcony. From a distance you looked really young and pretty, but now that I see you up close, I see that you are neither."

How was I supposed to respond to such a nasty comment? Not wanting to start a catfight right there in front of everyone, I responded, "That's a very interesting observation." At least I wasn't thanking her for her comment. However, my answer was not what she expected to hear, so she repeated herself, saying the same hurtful words. Realizing I was not going to win this battle I simply responded, "Thank you."

The wife who said she always needed to correct her husband, as well as the woman who felt compelled to give her assessment of my looks, both did so under the guise of "honesty." I'm always a little suspicious of a person who wants to do something that is unkind and hurtful yet all the while cloaks it in a shroud of righteousness. There is most assuredly something else going on.

The tactic of seeming to be virtuous while not acting in a godly manner is not that uncommon. In fact, we have several key examples of that behavior demonstrated in the Bible. In

1 Samuel chapter 15, God told Saul to annihilate the horribly wicked Amalekites. I realize this command for drastic violence offends our modern sensibilities, but I'm sure God had His reasons for such an action. King Saul was instructed to destroy all of the people and all of the animals. However, he only partially obeyed the Lord. Now, before you assume that Saul just didn't have the heart to hurt innocent people, remember that Saul did in fact kill all the men and women, children and infants, and most of the livestock. However, he spared the life of the wicked king and the most valuable of the animals.

When the prophet Samuel came to Saul and asked him if he had obeyed God, Saul assured him that he had done just as commanded. It was then that Samuel said, "What then is this bleating of the sheep in my ears, and the lowing of the oxen which I hear?" (verse 14). Saul said, "I did obey the voice of the LORD, and went on the mission on which the LORD sent me, and have brought back Agag the King of Amalek, and have utterly destroyed the Amalekites. But the people took some of the spoil, sheep and oxen, the choicest of the things devoted to destruction, to sacrifice to the LORD your God at Gilgal" (verses 20-21). Samuel went on to reveal the eternal truth that God desires obedience more than sacrifice.

Saul's dishonesty became apparent when he tried to make the case that he had not *really* disobeyed God, but that he wanted to use the spoils to make a wonderful, spiritual sacrifice to Him. His attempt to cleverly cloak his unholy actions is the same sin that we, in this modern age, are capable of committing. Whether it is hiding behind disobedience and justifying it as a spiritual act or using the excuse of "honesty" to justify unkind words and attitudes of anger, too often we do the same. How many of us are guilty of elevating to a virtue the idea of being uncontrollably, unreservedly honest with our thoughts and words? Instead, we are guilty of not admitting to ourselves that our rude and hurtful comments are not right and, if delivered, would be untimely and inappropriate.

I once heard a woman comment, "By my nature, I'm a forthright, speak-my-mind person. It's just in my character to be honest." This woman may not be necessarily driven by anger, but I assure you, because she has provoked others, she has many angry people in her life. Here again is someone who defined her uncontrolled (and often unsolicited) comments as a godly quality, or as "just doing what comes naturally"!

That lady, like the rest of us, should ask, "Since when is doing what comes naturally a good thing?" The very world around us cries out for restraint. We spend our lives fighting back what is natural. We mow our lawns, brush our teeth, use deodorant, comb our hair, diet, and exercise. None of those good and rightful things come automatically to us. We have to consciously choose the better over the natural. It is a good thing to fight our natural impulses to do and say the first thing that comes to our minds. If this is true, what makes us think that following our nature (which is basically sinful) is always the right thing to do? Romans 7:18 clearly states, "For I know that nothing good dwells in me, that is, in my flesh; for the wishing is present in me, but the doing of the good is not." I have found that in order for me to avoid the error of following my nature, I have to be constantly pulling the ugly weeds of misguided anger from the soil of my heart.

Speaking of weeds, I love to garden. I inherited that passion from my mother. Actually, calling myself a gardener is being rather generous with the term. I grow flowers. My mother was the real horticulturist. She was the one who could coax a tomato plant to grow in the middle of the Mojave Desert. Her labor was especially enjoyed by many in her family because she provided vegetables for all of her city-dwelling children.

I recall going home for visits and finding my mother in the garden with hoe in hand, fighting the weeds that sought—at the slightest chance—to take over her crop. Mom is now with the Lord, and I deeply miss her gifts of fresh vegetables. And, because neither she nor my father are there anymore, I don't get back to West Virginia very often. But not too long ago, I ventured a return to the old home place. There, where mom had spent untold hours keeping the weeds away, was a plot of ground unrecognizable as a garden except for the fence that marked the perimeter. The weeds stood as tall as a grown man. The message was clear. Nothing testifies to the destructive power of nature more than a plot of ground that was once cultivated but then left vacant.

Our lives are like gardens. If we want to have a peaceful, productive life, free from the life-stealing weeds of anger, we have to constantly be in the fight against our natural tendencies.

When it comes to the area of marriage, we especially have plenty of opportunities to resist our natural leaning toward brutal honesty and instead choose words and actions of love. When Steve and I are traveling on the road, presenting concerts and conducting marriage seminars, or when I speak at ladies' conferences and he accompanies me, we spend a lot of time in airplanes and rental cars. After a long day of traveling and ministering, it is so irritating to finally be on our way to our place of lodging, only to have Steve miss the exit to our hotel. Over the years I have developed a huge callous on my tongue from having to bite it. When I'm tired, it is especially hard for me to control my feelings of anger and frustration. (Of course, my little tirades offer Steve a chance to resist the urge to speak his mind when I choose to *not* resist saying hurtful things to him. I'm just trying to help him in his pursuit of maturity. Yeah, right!)

Before I finish my trip-to-the-hotel story, I must interject that exercising the restraint of saying something that may be true but hurtful is not the same as "bottling up our anger." Self-control is a mark of spiritual maturity, while giving the "silent treatment," on the other hand, denotes the exact opposite. By simply sitting on the lid of the container of anger we have accomplished nothing, and the rage stands ready to erupt at the first twist of the cap.

When my first response is to call Steve an incompetent idiot for his failure to get us to our hotel, I have to quickly ask myself some questions: *Just how accurate is my sense of direction? Could I find my way around a town I've never been in before? Do I really think Steve deliberately missed the exit? Do I think he is also tired, and perhaps that's why he missed the turn?*

Instead of allowing my natural tendency for an outburst of "angst" to flow freely, I do us both a favor and bite my tongue by either saying nothing or trying to help him navigate the interstate. Many times, after settling down and becoming a navigator instead of a "nag-igator," I am often the one who sees the exit we need because I'm busy helping instead of "harping."

Sometimes I do what is right, but I must admit there are other times when I go ahead and pull the trigger of my guns that are loaded with rage. It is in those instances when Proverbs 29:11 comes to mind: "A fool gives full vent to his anger, but a wise man keeps himself under control" (NIV).

Honestly Coming to Grips with Anger

I have alluded to the proposition that honesty is not always the best policy. I'm not suggesting we formulate some lie about an issue that has caused some level of tension. I am proposing, instead, that if our feelings can't be delivered with the right spirit and motive, then we should be quiet and wait until we are able to be gently honest.

The question is, then, "Is honesty ever a good policy?" The answer is, "Yes it is, as long as we honestly address the following three questions:

1. Is it true?
2. Is it kind?
3. Is it necessary?

In the chapter that follows, these important questions are addressed. I'm confident you will find further help in learning how to let honesty be your friend and not your foe.

8

Stop Horsing Around and Bridle Your Tongue!

"But let every one be quick to hear, slow to speak and slow to anger;
for the anger of man does not achieve the righteousness of God.
...If any one thinks himself to be religious, and yet does not bridle his tongue
but deceives his own heart, this man's religion is worthless."

—JAMES 1:19-20,26

As mentioned in the previous chapter, there are times when an honest assessment of a matter would best be held quietly in the heart. In other words, it would be wise to "take captive every thought to make it obedient to Christ" (2 Corinthians 10:5 NIV). The fortunate result will be the accomplishment of one of the greatest challenges known to mankind—that is, controlling the tongue. Most of us know very well that an unbridled tongue not only can ruin our lives, but can also ruin the lives of those around us. Proverbs 18:21 speaks about the incredible power of our words: "Death and life are in the power of the tongue."

Dr. D. L. Moody said:

> The tongue can be an instrument of untold good or incalculable evil. Someone has said that a sharp tongue is the only edged tool that grows keener with constant use. Bishop Hall said that the tongues of busybodies are like the tails of Samson's foxes—they carry firebrands and are enough to set the whole field of the world in flame. Blighted hopes and blasted reputations are witness to the tongue's awful power. In many cases the tongue has murdered its victims. Can we not all recall cases where men and women have died under the wounds of calumny and misrepresentation?[1]

A friend of mine told me that in the heat of an angry exchange with her husband, he said to her, "You could castrate a man with your tongue faster than someone could with a knife." This husband knew very well that the power of life and death is in the tongue.

If the tongue becomes an agent of our anger, we will surely wield the death blow to those we love as we mow them down with our words. In light of the seriousness of this truth, remember the three questions we must ask ourselves when deciding if we should say something:

1. Is it kind?
2. Is it true?
3. Is it necessary?

All three of these should be answered with an affirmative *before* we speak. Unfortunately, far too often we blast forth our feelings and observations without examining what unkind effect our verbiage might have on the hearer. Furthermore, we sometimes try to justify our gossip by saying, "But it's the truth!" However, just because something is not a lie does not mean it should be said. And to speak without any consideration given to whether or not our comment is necessary can be a grave mistake.

God has much to tell us about how we should and shouldn't use our tongues and the responsibility we will pay when we use them unwisely. In Psalm 59:7 David was crying out for God to protect him from Saul and the men who wanted to kill him. We read, "Behold, they belch forth with their mouth; swords are in their lips." Psalm 59:12-13 pronounces why the pursuers were doomed: "On account of the sin of their mouth and the words of their lips, let them even be caught in their pride, and on account of curses and lies which they utter. Destroy them in wrath."

The sins of their mouths, the careless words of their lips, and their angry curses were sins that made them worthy of severe judgment. In light of this, it is important for us to take into account the power for both good and evil that is in the tongue.

Proverbs 6:16 tells us what God hates: "There are six things which the LORD hates, yes, seven which are an abomination to Him: Haughty eyes (pride), a lying tongue, and hands that shed innocent blood, a heart that devises wicked plans, feet that run rapidly to evil, a false witness who utters lies, and one who spreads strife among brothers." Notice that three of the seven things God hates are connected to the misuse of the tongue.

The following passages will shed more light on God's feelings concerning the use of our tongues. Please take the time to read them carefully:

> The mouth of the righteous flows with wisdom, but the perverted tongue will be cut out. The lips of the righteous bring forth what is acceptable, but the mouth of the wicked, what is perverted (Proverbs 10:31-32).

By the blessing of the upright a city is exalted, but by the mouth of the wicked it is torn down. He who despises his neighbor lacks sense, but a man of understanding keeps silent. He who goes about as a talebearer reveals secrets, but he who is trustworthy conceals a matter (Proverbs 11:11-13).

An evil man is ensnared by the transgression of his lips, but the righteous will escape from trouble. A man will be satisfied with good by the fruit of his words, and the deeds of a man's hands will return to him (Proverbs 12:13-14).

There is one who speaks rashly like the thrusts of a sword, but the tongue of the wise brings healing. Truthful lips will be established forever, but a lying tongue is only for a moment (Proverbs 12:18,19).

A gentle answer turns away wrath, but a harsh word stirs up anger. The tongue of the wise makes knowledge acceptable, but the mouth of fools spouts folly...A soothing tongue is a tree of life, but perversion in it crushes the spirit (Proverbs 15:1,2,4).

The wise in heart will be called discerning, and sweetness of speech increases persuasiveness....The heart of the wise teaches his mouth, and adds persuasiveness to his lips (Proverbs 16:21,23).

He who goes about as a slanderer reveals secrets, therefore do not associate with a gossip (Proverbs 20:19).

He who guards his mouth and his tongue, guards his soul from troubles (Proverbs 21:23).

Strength and dignity are her clothing, and she smiles at the future. She opens her mouth in wisdom, and the teaching of kindness is on her tongue (Proverbs

31:25-26). (This does not sound like an angry woman. She is smiling! She knows when to open her mouth to speak, and when she does speak, it is kindness that comes out. What a great example of bridling the tongue!)

Even secular science has come to see what God has known all along. His wisdom found in Proverbs 15:1, "A gentle answer turns away wrath," was confirmed when The Speech Research Unit of Kenyon College proved through tests that when a person is shouted at, he or she simply cannot help but shout back.[2] You can use this scientific knowledge to keep another person from becoming angry by controlling the other person's tone of voice by your own voice. Psychology has proved that if you keep your voice low, you will not become angry. Psychology has accepted as scientific the old biblical injunction, "A soft answer turns away wrath." And even an old Chinese proverb supports this truth: "If you have a soft voice, you don't need a big stick."

In James 3:2 we are told that if "anyone does not stumble in what he says, he is a perfect man able to bridle the whole body as well." The reference to the bridle, a device used on the head of a horse to control its movement, makes the implication clear. If we can control our tongue the way a rider directs a large animal the size of a horse, then the discipline required to regulate the rest of our lives comes easier.

So that we are sure to get the message, James carried the equestrian picture a little further in verse 3: "Now if we put the bits into the horses' mouths so that they may obey us, we direct their entire body as well." I asked a lady who regularly works with horses about the usage of a bit. She informed me that while the bridle is placed over the horse's head, the bit is placed inside the horse's mouth, especially in the early stages of training.

Because of the pain that the hard metal appliance inflicts when the rider pulls the reins, the horse soon gets the message that it must obey. Eventually, she said, a horse may not require such measures. It will react to even the slightest pressure and show an obedient attitude. In the same way, our mouths must be trained to be responsive to the pressure of the Holy Spirit so that we can be submissive to Him when it comes to our words.

When we see the word "bridle" in this passage, many of us wrongly assume it is a mandate to never speak. That conjecture is not true. The horse's bridle is used for other purposes. It is used to slow an animal or to redirect it as it moves ahead. "If the Holy Spirit has control of this most volatile and intractable part of our being, how much more susceptible to His control will the rest of our lives be?"[3]

There is a question worthy of asking in regard to our tongues: Why are our words so important? It is because they reveal what we are thinking. "For as he thinks within himself, so he is" (Proverbs 23:7). And consider the familiar, "For out of the abundance of the heart the mouth speaks" (Matthew 12:34b NKJV). In light of these profound passages, I want my words to be pleasant as honeycomb, sweet to the soul and healing to the bones (see Proverbs 16:24). I desperately *don't* want them to be the sword that slashes and thrusts into the very soul of those I love. We are not only told that the tongue must be bridled, but we are also warned in James 3:8 that it is "a restless evil and full of deadly poison." Someone even called the tongue a shovel that can bury us under the negative attitudes and pronouncements of our lips. May it never be. There is hardly anything that will reveal that we have an anger problem more quickly than the words that come out of our mouths. Proverbs 4:23 instructs, "Watch over your heart with all diligence, for from it flow the springs of life. Put away from you a deceitful mouth, and put devious lips far from you." Proverbs 17:4 says, "An evildoer listens to wicked lips, a liar pays attention to a destructive tongue."

If the tongue is a tattletale of what our hearts and minds are contemplating, then how do we change our thinking, so that in turn we can pray, "Let the words of my mouth and the meditation of my heart be acceptable in Thy sight, O LORD, my rock and my Redeemer" (Psalm 19:14)?

Sometimes we try to change our thinking by saying, "I'm not going to have any more bad thoughts," and we concentrate on not saying what we shouldn't. Unfortunately, most of the time we end up saying the wrong thing anyway. I know this to be true by experience.

One day Steve and I went to visit a friend. We were very conscious that this person's father had committed suicide just a few months before. Being very aware of the sensitive nature of the death and the very recent grief our friend was experiencing, we went into the visit repeating to one another, "Be sure you don't bring up his father's death, and especially don't mention suicide." We also spent the evening individually rehearsing in our minds what we would *not* say.

We had a wonderful visit and we were standing at the door getting ready to leave. We continued making small talk, and, to be honest, we were very relieved that we had not created any embarrassing gaffes in our conversation that evening. Just before walking off the man's porch and heading home, Steve told our friend that we would be taking the toll road home that evening. As a parting comment, Steve turned and said, "I hate to travel the turnpike because it is so curvy and there have been so many serious accidents lately. When they give me that little ticket at the toll booth entrance, I feel like they are giving me a *suicide* note." The word "suicide" hung in midair like a wrecking ball, and Steve and I just stood there like a couple of old, vacant buildings.

All was awkwardly silent for a painfully long moment. We then bowed our heads and left. It was as if our minds were so saturated with what *not* to say, we just had to say it. I can't tell you how many times this very thing has happened.

In the same way, trying to not have angry thoughts is rather counterproductive. The better tactic by far is to replace the negative talk and futile thinking with God's thoughts, which are expressed in Philippians 4:6-8:

> Be anxious for nothing, but in everything by prayer and supplication with thanksgiving let your requests be made known to God. And the peace of God, which surpasses all comprehension, shall guard your hearts and your minds in Christ Jesus. Finally, brethren [sistren], whatever is TRUE, whatever is HONORABLE, whatever is RIGHT, whatever is PURE, whatever is LOVELY, whatever is of GOOD REPUTE, if there is any EXCELLENCE and if anything WORTHY OF PRAISE, let your mind dwell on these things (all caps mine).

How do we control our tongues and use our words to bring healing and life to those around us? We change how we think and what we think about. Sound simple? Yes. Is it easy? No! And it takes a lifetime to accomplish. Romans 12:1-2 is a familiar passage that many of us have read, reread, memorized, and posted all over our homes. However, presenting ourselves as living sacrifices and being conformed to the image of Christ, even as we are having our minds renewed daily, is no doubt the greatest challenge any of us will ever face.

There are those who are ahead of us in the journey to control what we say and how we say it. However, we must not become discouraged when we see others who may be lovely and sweet-talking while we are still struggling to not say cutting remarks to our husbands and children. When we see someone else's spiritual progress, it can be disheartening to think that they have arrived when we haven't even left the harbor. I saw a picture of this last Thanksgiving when we had all of Steve's family over for our holiday dinner. In the years past, Steve's mother had cooked many of the dinners, as had his sister, Jeannie. This past year was my turn. I worked and planned for weeks. I had my menu set, the grocery list recorded, and every task was meticulously scheduled for a particular day. When Thanksgiving Day arrived, I had most of the work done and dinner was ready when the family arrived at 12 o'clock sharp. As Heidi helped with the cleanup, she said something to me in a noticeably concerned voice: "Mom, you make it look so easy."

I knew what she was thinking. She would someday be married, and she was well aware that right now there was no way she could cook and serve a holiday dinner for 18 people. I could tell she felt defeated and I answered with great compassion. "Heidi, do you know who cooked the turkey when I was twenty?"

"No," she answered.

"My mom cooked the Thanksgiving dinner. Now that Mom is gone, I do the cooking. It took me all these years to learn how to serve a large group of people. When it's time for you to do the dinner, you'll know how because you will learn how to do it, one step at a time."

We look at saints of God who have walked with Him for decades, and they seem to have it all together. They make it look so easy. However, they have had many years of communing with God and ingesting His Word, thus allowing Him to change their ways of thinking. We must keep in mind that we are all a work in progress. Some have come farther than others, while some have had to overcome tremendous obstacles.

The Power of Words

A careless word may kindle strife
A cruel word may wreck a life
A bitter word may hate instill
A brutal word may smite and kill

A gracious word may smooth the way
A joyous word may light the day
A timely word may lessen stress
A loving word may heal and bless

—Author unknown

9

Hug in and Hold on: Drawing Near to God

"Now to Him who is able to keep you from stumbling, and to make you stand in the presence of His glory blameless with great joy, to the only God our Savior, through Jesus Christ our Lord, be glory, majesty, dominion, and authority, before all time now and forever. Amen."

—JUDE 1:24-25

One of life's most perplexing questions is addressed in the book of James: "What is the source of quarrels and conflicts among you?" (James 4:1). Haven't you asked yourself this same question? In the infamous Rodney King case where the race riots erupted in South Central Los Angeles, Mr. King pleaded, "Can't we all just get along?" I wish the answer to that question was easy. Unfortunately, it is not. But the good news is that the remedy for the anger which produces the divisive conflicts and quarrels among us is found in the Bible: "Submit therefore to

God. Resist the devil and he will flee from you. Draw near to God and He will draw near to you. Cleanse your hands, you sinners; and purify your hearts, you double-minded" (James 4:7-8).

It is important to note that there is an order to be followed in this passage. Without this biblical progression we might miss the answer to how we can avoid the effects of anger that erupt in hostility and strife with those around us. It is not a mistake that first on the list, we must **submit to God**. The literal meaning for the word "submit" is a military term meaning "to rank under." We voluntarily put ourselves under God's command even as a private in the Army willingly places himself under the command of a general.

Instead of letting anger be the commander of our responses, we give that control to God. To the degree that we trust Him and believe that He is in charge of all the things that touch our lives, it is to that level that we can accept the aggravations and irritations that are produced by dwelling among other humans.

Many of us have read the directives of this scripture and passed over the first part and immediately jumped to the second command, "Resist the devil." However, without first submitting to God, trying to combat spiritual darkness will get us in real trouble. An example of this mistake is found in the book of Acts, chapter 19. The seven sons of the Jewish chief priest Sceva, saw the tremendous power exhibited through the ministry of Paul. They wanted to tap into that power of expelling demonic spirits. They spoke to a demon-possessed man they were trying to set free and said, "I adjure you by Jesus whom Paul preaches" (verse 13). The response given by the demon in the man is very shocking: "And the evil spirit answered and said to them, 'I recognize Jesus, and I know about Paul, but who are you?' And the man, in whom was the evil spirit, leaped on them and subdued all of them and overpowered them, so that they fled out of that house naked and wounded" (verses 15-16). I would not have wanted to be the one the demon turned to in that moment and inquired, "Who are you?" It chills me to the bone to imagine it! Christ defeated Satan once and for all on the Cross. It is in His authority and power alone that we can resist the devil, but only *after* we have submitted to God.

The trouble comes when we submit to Him but fail to resist the devil. The result is that we stay defeated. On the other hand, if we reverse the order and resist the devil but don't submit to God, we will be both defeated and even more vulnerable to the schemes and attacks of the enemy.

There is great encouragement regarding our opportunity to put ourselves in God's mighty hand when it comes to dealing with the devil. It is found in Proverbs 3:5-8: "Trust in the LORD with all your heart, and do not lean on your own understanding. In all your ways acknowledge Him, and He will make your paths straight. Do not be wise in your own eyes; fear the LORD and turn away from evil. It will be healing to your body, and refreshment to your bones." With these weapons in our arsenal, we can go forth in boldness toward finding an end to the quarrels.

In an earlier chapter, I wrote about the physical effects that bitterness had on the health of my body and mind. I must add that a *lack of trust* in God will also hinder our ability to cope with all the little nuisances of life that contribute to living in a state of constant irritation. But most of us know that learning to trust God takes time and patience. It is not uncommon for a person given to a quick temper to be a very impatient person. These folks only add miles to their road toward trusting God. In James 5:7 we read of the farmer who knows the necessity of letting time produce mature crops. The same is true when we allow God to produce patience, a fruit of the Spirit, in our lives. We must remember that a crop is sown and grown through time. Managing the anger that seeks to take us over the line into sin also takes time. As we submit to God, it allows the fruit of the Spirit to mature in our hearts and lives.

Secondly, after submitting to God, we can then **resist the devil**. How do we do that? Do we sit around and constantly rebuke Satan? Do we seek out a pastor or an exorcist to pray for our spiritual deliverance? It is a valid question to ask "how" to resist the evil one. To find out, let's look at how Jesus dealt with the enemy.

Immediately after the baptism of Jesus, as recorded in Mark 1:12, the Spirit of God impelled Him into the wilderness to be tempted by Satan. The word for "impelled" is the Greek word *ekballo* which indicates the necessity of Jesus' testing. The temptation was coming from Satan, but it was part of God's plan to prepare His Son for the important work He had before Him.

The fourth chapter of Matthew gives some further details concerning the tempting of Christ by the devil. Time and time again, Satan would offer his best to Jesus, but each time it was rejected through the use of the Word of God. "It is written…" became the weapon Jesus used. Following His example, the Word of God is the same weapon we can use to fight against the enemy. The problem arises when we have not equipped our ammunition depot. Without taking the time and effort to fill our minds and hearts with His Word, we will find ourselves virtually defenseless in those times of temptation. The more submitted we are to God and the more we allow His Word to be sown and take root in our hearts, the better we can resist the devil. Furthermore, the more His word is in us, the less room there is for anger. Life is simple, but it's not easy! (For some of you, right now may be a good time to put this book aside and go find your Bible. Otherwise, the battle might be lost.)

Thirdly, after submitting and resisting, we are to **draw near to God**. There is a very good reason to do so, and it is well-illustrated by something I had to do when I was growing up on my parents' dairy farm in West Virginia. We milked cows each morning and evening, and these beasts had powerful hind legs that could do some significant physical harm if they connected with a kneecap or a jawbone. Some of the cows were docile and easy to manage. They were pleasant to work with because they did not kick at the person milking them. However, there were two kinds of cows that were dangerous to milk.

When a cow had "dropped" her calf (given birth, for you city folk), her udder would soon become tender and swollen with the excess milk. Any woman who has ever lactated and nursed a baby knows how uncomfortable the breast can become shortly after delivering.

Those poor old cows with their tender teats would then have to have automated milking machines attached to them. Often the udders would become infected with mastitis, causing terribly infected milk ducts. If we did not empty out the udders and relieve the pressure they could actually split open and the cow would be lost. Despite the pain, those poor old mamas had to be milked.

The other kind of cows that were dangerous were the mean ones that just didn't want to be bothered. They were usually the young heifers who were nervous and unfamiliar with the milking process.

Whenever I would attempt to milk either type of these difficult—and dangerous—cows I was risking my physical well-being. Oddly enough, I found that if I stayed back from them because of a fear of being kicked, I had a greater chance of being injured. What was necessary was for me to get as close to the cow as possible. I would literally wrap my arms around their middle section and hug in tightly. As long as I stayed close, I discovered, she was far less likely to hurt me.

When I read the admonition of James 4:7-8, as well as numerous other passages telling me to draw near to God, I recall how "hugging in and holding on" to the body of those bovines would spare me from a lot of unnecessary pain. Borrowing from that picture, as long as I stay close to God, I will not be harmed when the deadly hooves of anger are flying.

Fourthly, once we begin to draw near to our Holy God, something becomes very apparent as we stand in the light of His sinless majesty. We can look at ourselves and easily see that we need to **cleanse our hands of sin**. This has to do with the activities in which we engage. We are to put away the actions that are not holy. This may include changing the kind of materials we read, the part of the Internet we consume, the people with whom we associate, and—by all means—what we choose to indulge in when it comes to entertainment such as movies. A great guideline, by the way, for partaking in whatever Hollywood has to offer is to ask ourselves a probing question before we go to the theater: Would I find Jesus sitting in the seats at this movie? I have no doubt that if we honestly answered that question, we would rarely—if ever—go to another worthless flick. I realize this might present a challenging social sacrifice for some, but it is impossible to truly submit to God, resist the devil, and draw near to our Holy God without changing the way we live and the things we do.

Along with the cleansing of our activities, our hands may be dirtied by an offense we have committed toward another person. The purification of the hands may entail a humbling of one's self by going to the offended person and asking for forgiveness as well as—if possible—making restitution for the wrong things we said or did. We have a responsibility to remove any offense that we have done, therefore making it more possible for the offender to come to a place of peace. Once again I ask, "Does this advice sound simple?" Perhaps so. Is it easy? Of course not!

Fifthly, if **cleansing our hands** requires changing the things we do, then to **purify our hearts** means we must deal with the serious error of being **double-minded**. In other words, we have to change the way we think. Simple? Yes, but not easy! The reason our hearts are not pure is because we have minds that embrace the ways of both God and man. Isaiah 55:8-9 says, "'For My thoughts are not your thoughts, neither are your ways My ways,' declares the LORD. 'For as the heavens are higher than the earth, so are My ways higher than your ways, and My thoughts than your thoughts.'" This passage gave birth to a song lyric written by my husband, Steve. Note how his struggle with anger led him to an understanding about God that brought him to a place of submission.

You Have Your Ways, I Have Mine[1]

I admit I've been angry
I have not been happy for awhile
Ever since you changed my plans
It's been so hard to smile

But I can say I'm finished with the questions
I'm going to face the truth at hand
I know I'm only human
And there's some things in this life
I'll never understand

You have Your ways
I have mine
They'll never be the same
In all of time
We're not different in degree
We're different in kind
You have Your ways
And, I have mine.

Matthew 6:24 plainly says, "No one can serve two masters; for either he will hate the one and love the other, or he will hold to one and despise the other." On many occasions I've come to realize just how far my heart is from the "purity of [complete] devotion to Christ" (2 Corinthians 11:3). It is in those times that I feel compelled to pray and surrender all that I have and am to Him. I start by listing all the things with which God has graced my life. I thank Him for those I love, for my home, and for all He has given me. But when it comes time to dedicate these treasures to Him, I have to confess that a double-mindedness arises. While I have one foot in His presence, the other is stepping on the wordly fear that He might take it all away. This apprehension is magnified when I hear stories like the one our friend Joe related to us.

We were sharing with him and his wife, Linda, about how we are all in the process of learning to entrust more and more of our lives to God. As we talked, Joe said, "I remember when I prayed and surrendered my farm to God. The next night was when my barn burned down." As he told the story, things got rather quiet for a moment. He then explained how he was able to at least save his horses and, as it turned out, the insurance money actually paid for him to replace the barn with a much nicer building than he'd had before.

In order to fully commit the things to God that are important to me, I invariably have to face my lack of belief that "the LORD is [my] keeper" (Psalm 121:5). But I am always driven back to knowing that "without faith, it is impossible to please Him, for he who comes to God must believe that He is, and that He is a rewarder of those who seek Him" (Hebrews 11:6). I do believe that God "is." That's the first step in pleasing Him. But then I must believe that He is a rewarder of those who "crave" Him. Do I believe God is a "rewarder" or a "subtracter"? The more I pondered this, the more I thought about my children. If they were eating only chocolate cake, my love for them would require me to take away the pastry and give them some vegetables to eat. Why would I take away the cake? Because I know that eating only sweets would rot their teeth, give them soft bones, and make them fat and immobile. It would be only out of great love and concern that I would ever subtract from their lives. But I would always be giving something back in its place. Just as I would be careful to fulfill my children's needs, God does the same for His own.

To sum up, I am confident that no one really thinks we can live in this world and avoid the emotion of anger. Truth is, I think most of us would agree it would be irksome to be around a person who is incapable of experiencing anger. That individual would probably be rather impassionate, even boring, to be around.

Anger is simply going to be a natural part of living in a fallen world. In fact, we are given a license to feel anger in the familiar two-part verse found in Ephesians 4:26. The first admonition is, "Be angry..." There are indeed some current issues we should feel angry about, such as the atrocity of abortion, child and spouse abuse, corruption in government, and the harsh persecution of fellow believers in this country and other nations. When we are angry over the miscarriage of righteousness, we are reflecting the very character of God. It is commendable.

The second part of the verse is "…and yet do not sin." How could we possibly accomplish this command in the face of the injustices that we see? In order to avoid slipping into the sin-side of anger, may we not forget the way of escape found in the same verse: "…do not let the sun go down on your anger." By limiting the duration of your wrath and restricting its destructiveness ("Do not give the devil an opportunity") we are able to give the appropriate response, which is expressing anger, and yet not fall into sin.

May we always, "**submit** therefore to God. **Resist** the devil and he will flee from you. **Draw near** to God and He will draw near to you. **Cleanse your hands**, you sinners; and **purify your hearts**, you **double-minded**." And may we always "hug in and hold on" to God!

10

Anger and Marriage

*"For the eyes of the Lord are upon
the righteous, and His ears
attend to their prayer…"*

—1 PETER 3:12

Vanessa was just 20 years old, but she knew exactly what she wanted. She was going to get married, have a wonderful romance-filled life, and live happily ever after. Five years later she found herself living in a small apartment in a town far away from family and friends. With no access to a phone, television, or car, she spent her days with a colicky baby who cried incessantly. Finding herself weighing 80 pounds more than when she got married, she was one angry person.

Screams of rage replaced the sweet talk of the dating days, and sexual favors were withheld as punishment for a non-attentive husband. What happened to cause such extreme hostility in the life of this young woman?

The anger problem started long before the discovery that her man was not as romantic as she'd previously thought. Her rage was established well before the financial stress or the demanding baby. The impasse began years earlier when, as a teenage girl, Vanessa's seeds of rebellion were sown. Raised in the home of loving Christian parents, Vanessa wanted to please them, yet the pull of the world tugged at her heart. She found herself living a life of deception. Publicly she followed the rules that were expected of a deacon's daughter, and yet her conduct, as it pertained to her personal life, created a scenario of guilt and self-loathing.

Vanessa was in this state of mind when she met a young fellow she thought was worthy of her love and devotion. She fell for him, even if it meant forsaking her dreams of a career and independence. He lavished her with words of flattery and constant praise for her beauty and grace. Enticing promises of a lifetime of companionship and financial security soon turned her head and directed her into marriage.

Dedicated to selfish indulgences, her fellowship with God grew distant and impersonal. As a result, Vanessa shrunk back from sincerely seeking God's guidance concerning her life choices and plans. Before she could get all the wedding rice out of her hair, her husband's complimentary words abruptly ceased. They were replaced with grunts and demands for food and sex. As it became more and more clear that her husband's focus was totally on his own ambitions and needs, she began to resent being so young and tied down. Hers was a marriage that was not living up to its promised expectations. Her disappointment, lack of contentment, and isolation soon led to regret and seething rage.

"When we were out in public," she told me, "everyone thought we were just a sweet young couple. But when I was home, I turned into a crazy, raging person. I would get in my husband's face and scream, 'You tricked me into marrying you. You turned my head with words, and now life is nothing the way you promised it would be. I hate you!'"

Vanessa and her husband were locked into a difficult situation. They each blamed the other for their unhappiness. The husband accused her of deceiving him because he had no idea she was even capable of such out-of-control outbursts of rage. He was shocked at how mean and cruel she could be. On the other hand, she blamed him for everything, especially her sense of unhappiness. And each condemned the other for the sexual sin in which they had indulged before they married. Having violated what they both knew was God's directive concerning purity, they were reaping the consequences of ignoring it. As a result, they were experiencing the painful truth that sin never unites; it always divides. And that division, which results from sexual immorality, was tearing them apart. Consequently, both Vanessa and her husband were feeling angry and unloved. They were withholding what each one needed and desired.

Like Vanessa, another friend, Doris, was having a difficult time dealing with hurt feelings and outbursts of anger. As soon as I met her, I realized she was a woman who had been deeply wounded. She was a lovely, sensitive, and obviously soul-starved woman who didn't know where to turn. When she was given the chance to talk, she did so with great intensity. As her words tumbled out, she acted as though she expected me to abruptly walk away from her at any moment. While sharing so deeply from her broken heart, she mentioned the pain of "not being heard." Although she had married a Christian man, her tremendous need for conversation and affection was not something her husband shared or even understood. Therefore, she lived in a marriage where she felt very alone.

When her husband's silence and indifference turned to outbursts of slamming remarks and verbal put-downs, she wondered where she could turn and to whom she could confide. Everyone loved and respected her husband, Jim. He was a wonderful Christian worker and an inspirational speaker. When Doris complained to the church authorities that Jim was neglecting her and their children, they reminded her of his busy schedule. She was told to adapt herself to his needs. When she confided in them that he was brutally unkind, moody, and unpredictable, she was met with disbelief. The very counselors she approached for help and support were the ones who took Jim's side and shamed her for her insensitivity to his needs. They threw a few Bible verses at her, told her what a wonderful husband God had blessed her with, and gave her a sermonette on the biblical role of the woman. As a result, she felt accused and shamed for her seeming lack of submission.

By the time I met her, the years of hurtful words and spiritual abuse had left Doris beaten down, depressed, and angry. However, it was curious that even in her weakened condition she would defend Jim. She would share some insensitive and sometimes downright nasty things he had said or done to her. But after so doing, she would quickly interject, "Oh, he's gotten so much better than he used to be. I don't want you to think ill of him; he's such a good man of God."

Even though I perceived Doris as an angry wife, I'm not sure she saw herself as hostile toward her husband. It is true that she wasn't ranting or screaming obscenities at Jim. However, her anger was unwittingly expressed by her frequent mentioning of her unmet needs.

Vanessa and Doris were each expressing anger in different ways. On one hand, Vanessa would get in her husband's face and scream, "I hate you! I wish you would die! I wish I had not married you!" On the other hand, Doris had tried to quietly pray and privately talk to a counselor, but eventually she learned that no one would help her. She was alone, and her anger took the form of resignation and depression.

Whether you identify with the "vocal Vanessa" or the "depressed Doris" or someone in between, anger in marriage takes its deadly toll. The sad end is that outbursts of anger are whips that many women use to punish their spouse. During a women's conference I asked the ladies to honestly share with me how and in what manner they used anger in an attempt to control, change, or chasten their husbands. These were some of their responses:

> *I use anger in an effort to get him to stop drinking and swearing. It makes me very angry when he acts like that. I try to "correct" his bad behavior through yelling, crying, and using the silent treatment. Sometimes I feel guilty that I use anger in this way, but I feel if I don't get it out, I'll explode.*

> *There are times when I say things to him that I know will hurt him. It's usually after he's hurt my feelings that I retaliate with screaming and yelling ugly things at him. Unfortunately, it doesn't seem to do any good, because he just pouts, sulks, and withdraws himself from me and the kids. His reaction keeps me feeling angry.*

Anger is difficult for me to deal with. My parents always fought and swore at each other. I promised myself I would never act like that. However, I find that I get so upset when I'm right and he won't admit that he's wrong. I feel he should know what's wrong with me when I'm silent. I want him to come and apologize to me, but he never does. A lot of our problems go unresolved because neither of us will talk about it.

I guess one reason I have an anger problem is because I just can't forget about the affair my husband had. I've forgiven him, but whenever something comes up that makes me mad, I tell him he has no right to treat me that way "because..." and he knows what that means. Sometimes I feel guilty that I keep bringing up his sin and rubbing his nose in it, but it just comes out. If I'm not yelling and arguing, then I'm giving him the silent treatment. I feel like no one wins in my marriage. He's miserable and I can't get over the past. Our only hope is going to be if God changes my heart, but my husband is going to have to try harder, too.

I get angry for no important reason. I think by now it's just a habit, a part of how I am. And when I get really mad, I don't think rationally. I lash out at my husband and say the most hurtful things to him. I'm constantly pointing out his shortcomings. I yell, curse, and even hit him sometimes. After I've "let go on him" I don't feel any better. In fact, debasing him and seeing the hurt on his face makes me feel worse. It's my goal to be a better Christian wife, mother, and just a nicer

person, but God is really going to have to help me. Right
now, I'm pretty out of control.

I feel like I can't restrain myself. I give my husband
the silent treatment until I start to cry. When he finally
comes to me and tries to make up, I turn him away. I feel
guilty because I don't handle my anger the way I should.
I think it hurts him the most when I say he's a bad father.
He didn't have a good dad, so this is how I can really get
to him. I know that's mean. I'm praying to do better.

I use angry outbursts to punish my husband. He
seems so strong, so when I feel like he's wounded me I
respond by hurting him with my words. The thing that
really cuts him to the bone is when I say, "I want a
divorce." He's gone through one previously so I say, "You
got a divorce before, you can do it again." He hates it
when I yell at him, but mostly he hates it when I shut
him out with the wall I build up inside me.

I know how to get back at my husband. I withhold
sex from him. That's when he knows I'm really mad. If
I want his attention and he doesn't give it to me, then I
push him away when he wants to make love. I know it
doesn't fix the problem, but somehow I feel as though I
have some power over him. Sometimes he looks so hurt,
I wonder if he wants sex, or if I've just really hurt his
feelings.

I get very angry when my husband doesn't help me
with the raising of the kids. I use a lot of sarcasm and
put-downs to get my point across. I make him feel guilty
for not helping me. It makes me angry that I have to go

to such measures to get him to be a good dad. I know I'm a perfectionist at times and I try to control the household, but that's not all my fault. My husband worked nights when the kids were little, so I had to take over and dominate things. But now he needs to help me more. He's really a nice person, and I feel badly that I'm so angry all the time.

I'm not doing very well in managing my anger. I yell, scream, and even use curse words that I know are wrong. I've even tried giving my husband the silent treatment, but I don't think it even bothers him at all. My angry outbursts make me feel horrible and guilty. I know I'm not acting like a good Christian. Some of the fault is on my husband because he doesn't give me any attention. In fact, the only thing he really notices is when I withhold sex from him. When his needs are not met, then he gets angry.

Using anger to get my husband's attention is all I've ever known. I yell, use stinging one-liners, and use the silent treatment. I feel so rejected and ignored that anger is a pressure valve that I need. I'm afraid if I didn't vent on him, I'd explode. Sometimes when I act angry, it puts me in control. In a strange way, everyone acts a little better toward me while I'm angry. However, I know it's not right. I can feel it breaking down the very core of our marriage. Anger stops the free flow of love between us. I wish I could find another, more positive way to get his attention.

It is obvious from the above statements that in some cases the things we do to reduce the pressure of pent-up rage work against the goal of feeling better and only increase the tension. In the same conference setting, I asked these ladies, "If there was one thing you could do to make the anger more manageable, what would it be?" Their responses were:

—If I could understand my past and forgive those who hurt me.

—If I had more order in my home. All the clutter around makes me crazy.

—If my husband would come back home and apologize for leaving me and my daughter.

—If I were physically healthy and not so tired. I need a less hectic schedule.

—If my spouse would acknowledge our problems. I need to know that he is listening to me and that he hears my heart.

—If I would be more patient with my family and learn to love unselfishly.

—If I would just accept that it's never going to be any different and my husband is never going to change as long as I'm the one who is trying to change him.

—If I had a closer walk with God and spent more time in prayer.

—If I had someone to tell me they loved me.

—*If I admitted to God and to myself when I'm angry. I keep blaming others for my outbursts. I need to learn to be honest.*

—*If I controlled my thoughts, I think my words would be nicer.*

—*If I would listen to the person I'm angry with. I want to be heard, but I also need to hear what they have to say.*

—*If I would think first, then talk it out with the Lord. When I stop and pray, the results are much better for everyone. My husband is the one working on controlling his anger. When I return anger, it makes matters worse.*

—*If I were more grateful for what I have.*

—*If my husband loved and cared for me.*

—*If I spent more time in the Word then I would be more aware of when I'm wrong.*

—*If those who offended me would apologize then maybe I could get over it.*

—*If my family would pick up after themselves and not depend on me to do it.*

—*If I would stop and think about how badly I'm going to feel after my angry outbursts.*

—*If I believed that Romans 12:19 were true and lived by the truth that vengeance belongs to God.*

—*If I could get away occasionally from the children and even my husband. I'm at such a disadvantage when I'm exhausted. I can't think straight when I'm sleep-deprived.*

—If I had someone to talk to, other than my spouse. I need someone else's perspective. Actually, I need adult contact during the day so I'm not so angry with my children.

—If I had more respect for the opinions of others.

—If I knew how to confront in a positive way. The problem is, I usually take it out on myself and I get depressed.

—If I could just lose all this weight I've gained.

These statements are not just the heart cries of women who are on the battlefield of anger, many of them are timely bits of wisdom said much better than I could say. The bottom line is, when it comes to anger and marriage, most of us know what to do to avoid the pitfalls of rage. *Whether or not we follow through is the question.* The good news is that there is comfort in knowing our pleas for help will not go unheard by the heavenly Father. We have the promise that if we ask we will receive, if we seek we will find, and if we knock it will be opened to us...for "your Father who is in heaven [gives] what is good to those who ask Him" (Matthew 7:11).

As a footnote, my time with the women at the previously-mentioned conference also yielded two other issues worthy of attention. The first was the matter of domestic violence. I was approached by a woman who asked for a private moment with me. As she tearfully revealed her very difficult situation at home, it occurred to me that she might have been speaking on behalf of some others who were in attendance, as well as some who may be reading these pages.

While this book is not written to address this tragedy, it must be mentioned because it is dangerous to keep silent about it. As I have talked to professional counselors who have sought to help women in violent marriages, they have told me that when a woman admits that the environment in which she lives is both immoral and displeasing to God, she takes the first step toward getting help to change things. The following lyric describes a hurting woman much like the one I spoke to that day:

Inside Story[1]

It's Sunday morning, it's 10 A.M.
The congregation is gathering in
And she smiles like the rest of the women and men
But inside, her heart is breaking.

'Cause her man showed his rage, again last night
But, like a martyr though, she didn't fight
And the wounds he gave her, she was able to hide
She comes around for a reason.

And she sits in the crowd alone, with the pain she hides so well
Wishing someone knew the inside story, she's so afraid to tell
She needs someone to talk to, to see the pain that's in her eyes
She needs someone who will listen
And to see through her disguise.

It's been a while, since she believed
That she's worth more than the pain he leaves

And she doesn't think much of the woman she sees
When she looks into the mirror
Now she's afraid of the man she loves
She blames herself for the things he does
Oh! How she wishes he'd be like he was
Back when his touch was tender.

And she sits in the crowd alone, with the pain she hides so
    well
Wishing someone knew the inside story, she's so afraid to tell
She needs someone to talk to, to see the pain that's in her eyes
She needs someone who will listen
And to see through her disguise.

Now they're singing the closing hymn
Soon they'll be saying the last "Amen."
And maybe next Sunday she'll come again
But she'll come around for a reason.

If this lyric represents your situation and your desire is to share your troubled heart with someone but saying the words would come much too hard, let me make the following suggestion. Copy the words and simply hand them to a trustworthy friend. After she reads them, look her in the eye and say, "That woman is me." At that moment the initial step to healing will have been taken. The next steps can be found by pursuing other resources, books, and organizations that expertly address this serious cause of your abiding anger.

The second issue that I encountered concerned some young single ladies who were present. When they heard the anonymous and frank admissions of others who were in extremely hurtful relationships, they seemed to show panic in their countenance. Some admitted they were looking forward to meeting and marrying "the one," but found the stories of these unhappy women to be discouraging. If you are a young single woman and feel this apprehension, it must be said that there is no guarantee that a Christian man will make you happy. However, let me urge you—please don't be turned away from pursuing a man of faith. Though there is no guarantee that choosing a Christian husband will secure your marital bliss, selecting a man who does not share your faith will *definitely* assure you of a life of disharmony in the most important and eternal area of your life—your walk with Christ. Second Corinthians 6:14 ("Do not be bound together with unbelievers...") testifies to this truth and is the basis for the following lyric.

If You Marry Across the Border[2]

In the land of True Believers
Lived a maiden young and fair
She would've made a good wife
To any young man living there
But a man from across the border
Won her heart and so it seemed
That they would marry though she knew well
It would not please her King.

For the King of all believers
Made it clear so long ago
If you marry across the border
Sorrow's all you'll marry for.

Still the maiden crossed on over
And while crossing she declared
I'll bring him back to where I'm from
It's been years and he's still there.

The King of all believers
Made it clear long ago
If you marry across the border
Sorrow's all you'll marry for.

The book of 1 Peter offers a perfect solution to the dangerous issue of marriage and anger.

> To sum it up, let all be harmonious, sympathetic, brotherly, kindhearted, and humble in spirit; not returning evil for evil, or insult for insult, but giving a blessing instead; for you were called for the very purpose that you might inherit a blessing. For, "let him who means to love life and see good days refrain his tongue from evil and his lips from speaking guile. And let him turn away from evil and do good; let him seek peace and pursue it. For the eyes of the Lord are upon the righteous, and His ears attend to their prayers but the face of the Lord is against those who do evil" (1 Peter 3: 8-12).

11

If Mama Ain't Happy…: Raising Angry Children

"She opens her mouth in wisdom,
and the teaching of kindness
is on her tongue."

—PROVERBS 31:26

Most anger rolls downhill. Very few of us vent our hostility on the more powerful people in our lives. If we are irritated with our boss, most often it is the worker on the lower rung of the ladder who catches it. Instead of barging into the executive suite and reaming out the CEO, the guy at the red light we encounter during the drive home—the one who takes a bit too long to move his car—is the one who receives our evaluation of his IQ. If it's not a person in our lives who is on the receiving end of our anger, it may be a car door that gets slammed or a poor little innocent dog that gets a swift kick. Even though we may be "madder than a wet hen," we still seem to have enough control to decide who "gets it." Most often we can curtail our anger if the police officer pulls us over for a broken taillight, but pity the unsuspecting husband who never got around to fixing it and is blamed for subjecting us to such humiliation.

It is because of this tendency to vent our rage on the weaker people in our lives that I felt compelled to address the topic of our children and the anger they receive and learn from us.

We are admonished throughout the scriptures that, as parents, we are to avoid the natural tendency of provoking anger in our children. Providing a safe, peaceful environment takes a conscious choice and diligent attention. However, annoying our kids seems to take little effort. For example, I'll never forget when Steve and Heidi returned from a canoe trip with some other parents and their children. They told me about the dad who spent the entire two days on the river correcting every move his daughter made. In the hollowness of the riverbed, where voices echo clearly for everyone to hear, the father tortured not only his daughter with his incessant complaints about her alleged incompetence, but the rest of the group was subjected to the sad scene as well. The young girl wept most of the trip down the quiet river. Her sobs were audible. That child knew firsthand about the ills of being provoked.

Damaging our children by presenting an atmosphere of constant bickering and hostility is not something that any of us as parents deliberately set out to do. No doubt the father of the little girl in the canoe did not look into the crib when she was an infant and say, "When you get older, I'm going to make your life miserable!" Instead, parents sometimes hurt children without intending to do it.

There is a helpful illustration of this truth found in 2 Samuel 4:4: "Now, Jonathan, Saul's son, had a son crippled in his feet. He was five years old when the report of Saul and Jonathan came from Jezreel, and his nurse took him up and fled. And it happened that in her hurry to flee, he fell and became lame. And his name was Mephibosheth." The Hebrew word for "fell" is *naphal,* which means "to be dropped." The main idea behind this root word is a violent or accidental circumstance or event. I found it very interesting that Mephibosheth was lame because someone who obviously cared for him and tried to protect him accidentally "dropped" him.

We don't hear about Mephibosheth again until the ninth chapter of 2 Samuel. Many years later, David was grieving over the loss of his friend Jonathan. He sought information concerning anyone who would be left as a descendent. David inquired, "Is there yet anyone left of the house of Saul, that I may show him kindness for Jonathan's sake?" (verse 1). A former servant of Saul was still in the palace. David asked Ziba if he knew of anyone related to Jonathan. It was at that time that David learned about Mephibosheth. He found out that the young man was living in Lo-Debar, so David sent a servant to bring him to the palace.

When Mephibosheth appeared before David, fearing for his life, he fell at the king's feet and prostrated himself, stating, "Here is your servant!" (verse 6). Both Mephibosheth and David were aware that it was customary for reigning kings to completely annihilate any descendants of the previous rulers to avoid an insurrection attempt. I'm sure Mephibosheth was dreading this very fate when David said, "Do not fear, for I will surely show kindness to you for the sake of your father Jonathan, and I will restore to you all the land of your grandfather Saul; and you shall eat at my table regularly" (verse 7).

This is very relevant to our lives as "crippled" people trying to parent our children. Granted, some of us were emotionally injured as a result of a deliberate act of violence. Consequently, it is much more difficult for us to effectively and compassionately love our kids. However, most of us have been accidentally "dropped" by our own parents or caretakers. But regardless of the source of harm, the results for all of us who are now moms may be a challenging struggle with anger to one degree or another. An eruptive personality may result from the past and may have "crippled" our relationship with our own children. In turn, the result is that they too are ridden with conflicts and problems. This is most unfortunate. For many of us, it is not a deliberate, hateful act toward our children that has caused them pain, but instead the harm that is borne out of our own unresolved offenses.

Not long ago I was talking to a 20-year-old woman who was having problems with her boyfriend. Actually, her dilemma was that she didn't want him to be her boyfriend any longer and she didn't know how to break up with him. Because they had had a "forever" talk and he thought she was more serious about him than she really was, she felt a certain amount of obligation to keep seeing him. While we were talking she expressed her misgivings about marrying this young man, but, more importantly, she expressed her disdainful attitude about marriage in general.

She confided, "I don't want to repeat the same mistakes my parents made. I don't want the kind of marriage they have. My life has been nothing but chaos with all their fighting and bickering."

This girl had been crippled emotionally. She had a terrible attitude and opinion of marriage because she had never really seen a happy relationship where people conduct themselves in a mature, adult-like manner and actually get along. Because of her childhood, she may spend her future limping along in the area of family because someone "dropped" her. In this case it was her parents. But they didn't harm her on purpose. She was unintentionally hurt because of their inability to deal constructively with their conflicts and angry feelings.

In the area of anger, as it relates to our children, I am reminded of Ephesians 6:4: "...fathers, do not provoke your children to anger; but bring them up in the discipline and instruction of the Lord." Actually, the word for "father" in the Greek is *pateres*, which can be translated to mean "parent." Since the previous passages involved both the mother and father, it is logical to conclude that the word *pateres* is referring to both parents. And in Colossians 3:21 we read, "Fathers [moms and dads], do not exasperate your children, that they may not lose heart." The word "exasperate" is the Greek word *erethizo,* which means "to stir up, provoke, irritate." We are not to provoke our children because they will "lose heart." The idea of losing heart is "to be listless, sullen, discouraged, despairing, without courage or spirit." I couldn't help but think how this description of a child who has "lost heart" sounds hauntingly like the generation of children who are so destructive to our culture with all of the school shootings and other acts of juvenile violence we see so prevalent today.

If provoking our children is forbidden by the Scriptures, what can we do to avoid it? In the interest of time and space, I want to address one of the most harmful ways a child can be irritated to the point of anger. As parents, we spend a lot of our time thinking about and working toward what we want to *give* our children. To the contrary, it is what we *don't give* to them that often leaves them disheartened. We exasperate our children and at times "drop them" by withholding the following things.

Withholding a Good Example

Children are not fools. We cannot, as their parents, tell them to live a certain way and yet live the opposite way ourselves. We can't get by with telling them, "Do as I say, not as I do." When we do, we provoke our children with our hypocrisy. It's important that we understand what a hypocrite is. According to Webster's dictionary, the word means, "One who is acting a part, pretending, feigning to be what one is not, a deception as to real character and feeling, especially in regard to morals and religion."[1]

Children are often best instructed by visual means. When I was in school I had a real problem with math. For some reason numbers and I just didn't add up. The most difficult part of arithmetic was the word problems. I could read the question over and over, yet I could never seem to grasp what I was supposed to do. However, if someone would go to the blackboard and work it out in front of me, it all seemed to make sense. I needed to *see* how to work the problem. In the same way, we can tell our kids all day long about faith and walking with God. But it would all seem unreal until our children *see* us walking it out in front of them. Then it will make sense.

I experienced a situation recently in which someone hurt me deeply and took advantage of me. My children were very much aware of the problem and were ready to take up the offense. They watched to see how I was going to deal with the circumstance. They observed as I humbled myself, forgave, and reached out to the offender. A few days after the problem was resolved, my son, Nathan, said, "I've heard about forgiveness all my life, and I've experienced it to a degree. Actually, I'm usually the one needing to be forgiven. But this time, I saw what living for Christ looks like. Mom, you've shown me what being a Christian really means."

To be honest with you, I knew my children were watching me, and I knew they would learn from my example whether all this "church talk" meant anything in the real world. Knowing I was being watched helped me make better choices than if I had had the luxury of feeding my hurt feelings and nursing a grudge. There was too much at stake to give in to my flesh.

We provoke our children by not being good examples of who God wants them to be and what He wants for their lives. This reminds me of a letter and cassette we received from a man whose daddy left him before he was born. This father abandoned his wife and children, provoking them to nearly lose all hope. Without Christ in their lives and a strong mother who was a good example, they never could have survived. Here are the words Steve wrote after listening to this man's story.

The Pocket[2]

Daddy left in January, and I was born in April
I was down the line, the last of nine and I'll be forever grateful
For the way my Momma stayed with us, and said our names
    to Jesus
Oh, but she was sad, she missed our dad and wondered why
    he'd ever leave us.

We didn't have a dime, but we were rich, and Mom was good
    at sewin'
She took a bag of old cut up rags, and before it started snowin'
She made a quilt to keep us warm, and I slept underneath it
And in the seams was Dad's old blue jeans among all the other
    pieces.

And then one night, I'll not forget, in that quilt I found a
    pocket
I remember what my Momma said, when I put my hand
    inside it
"The night your Daddy said 'goodbye' he left everything
    behind him
and where your hand is, he once had his," she left the room a
    cryin'.

So many nights I cried myself to sleep, underneath that cover
With my hand where his had been, back when he loved our
    mother
And sometimes those memories flood my soul, if I tried I
    couldn't stop it
Now that old quilt is gone, but I live on, with my hand inside
    that pocket.
Yes, my daddy's gone, but I live on, with my hand inside his
    pocket.

While the dad left the potential for a lifetime of scars and anger in the hearts of his children, the mother—on the other hand—provided the godly example they needed to emotionally survive. The son in this story is a testimony to her good example.

Withholding Boundaries

There are many examples of parents who provoked their children by withholding loving discipline. Hebrews 12:7-11 says:

> It is for discipline that you endure; God deals with you as with sons; for what son is there whom his father [or mother] does not discipline? But if you are without discipline, of which all have become partakers, then you are illegitimate children and not sons. Furthermore, we had earthly fathers to discipline us, and we respected them; shall we not much rather be subject to the Father of spirits, and live? For they disciplined us for a short time as seemed best to them, but He disciplines us for our good, that we may share His holiness. All discipline for the moment seems not to be joyful, but sorrowful; yet to those who have been trained by it, afterwards it yields the peaceful fruit of righteousness.

It seems that the reason withholding discipline causes anger in a child is that, eventually, the child comes to understand that it is a sign of a parent's lack of diligent love for them. Proverbs 19:18 says, "Discipline your son while there is hope, and do not desire his death." There are moms who have not disciplined their children, and as a result the children have turned into such monsters that the mothers don't want to live with them. Some Christian parents have medicated their children or turned them over to the foster care system when they find they cannot handle them any longer.

King David was a wonderful king, but he was a neglectful father who withheld discipline. In 2 Samuel chapter 13 we read about three of his children. If you carefully follow the story to its completion, you will see how a father's lack of discipline can lead to the destruction of all his children.

Absalom and Amnon were half-brothers. They each shared David as their father, but had two different mothers. Absalom had a full sister, Tamar. Amnon, 22 years old, was infatuated with Tamar, his 15-year-old half-sister. He desired her sexually.

You may be familiar with the story of how Amnon, along with his first cousin Jonadad, concocted a deception in which Amnon would feign sickness. When David saw his son seemingly ill, Amnon asked King David to send for Tamar to come tend to him. Amnon was the heir-apparent to the throne and obviously favored by David. David sent for Tamar to care for her brother and prepare him something to eat. She fixed the meal and gave it to him. He refused to eat and asked her to send everyone away.

He then lured her into his bedroom under the pretense that he needed her to feed him while he was lying in bed. When she came into his room "he took hold of her and said to her, 'Come, lie with me, my sister.' But she answered him, 'No, my brother, do not violate me, for such a thing is not done in Israel; do not do this disgraceful thing!'" (verses 11-12).

She tried to reason with him to wait. She said if he would only ask, their father would allow them to marry. Verse 14 says, "However, he would not listen to her; since he was stronger than she, he violated her and lay with her." The passage further reveals that after the assault was done, "Amnon hated her with a very great hatred; for the hatred with which he hated her was greater than the love with which he had loved her. And Amnon said to her, 'Get up, go away!'" (verse 15).

As we continue to read in verses 16-17: "But she said to him, 'No, because this wrong in sending me away is greater than the other that you have done to me!' Yet he would not listen to her. Then he called his young man who attended him and said, 'Now, throw this woman out of my presence, and lock the door behind her.'" Tamar was permanently marred and publicly disgraced by her brother.

When King David heard what Amnon had done to his very own daughter, the Scripture tells us he was "very angry" (verse

21). He might have been upset, but, surprisingly, he did nothing about it. He let Amnon get away with a scandalous, immoral, vile act without disciplining him in any way.

However, the offense did not go unnoticed by Tamar's brother, Absalom, then 23 years old. Absalom loved his sister. He took her into his own home and decided to take matters into his own hands. He waited two years before he sought his revenge against his brother. Absalom devised a scheme to get the sons of David together.

When the sheepshearers gathered to celebrate the harvesting of the wool, Absalom, host of the event, asked his father, David, and the king's sons to attend. After Absalom asked repeatedly for them to be present, David finally consented for Amnon and the rest of his sons to be at Absalom's party. Absalom gave instructions to his men to get Amnon "merry with wine" (verse 28) and then to kill him when he gave the word. Just as requested, at the appointed time Absalom's servants fell on Amnon and killed him. The rest of the brothers mounted their mules and fled for safety.

The report soon reached David that all his sons had been slain. Jonadad, the one who had devised the plan to assault Tamar, informed David the report was not factual. The only son who had died was Amnon. David was reunited with all his sons, except for Absalom, who fled to Geshur, the home of his maternal grandfather, and stayed there for three years. Instead of David disciplining Amnon, he let him go his sinful way. Likewise, David did not pursue Absalom, even though he had committed premeditated murder. One would have to wonder if David's reluctance to discipline his sons was influenced by his own sinful past.

David had committed adultery with Bathsheba and violated God's moral laws. Then David, with premeditation, had Uriah killed without mercy. Absalom had murdered a guilty man; David had murdered a man who was innocent and full of honor. David's own sordid past may very well have kept him from being the kind of father he needed to be. (At times, as parents we allow our own guilty consciences to influence our responsibility to set boundaries with our children.)

Regardless of the reason David neglected to discipline his sons, the results were disastrous. In 2 Samuel 12:10-12 the stinging pronouncement of the prophet Nathan sadly was fulfilled in the lives of David's own children.

> "Now therefore, the sword shall never depart from your house, because you have despised Me and have taken the wife of Uriah the Hittite to be your wife." Thus says the LORD, "Behold, I will raise up evil against you from your own household; I will even take your wives before your eyes, and give them to your companion, and he shall lie with your wives in broad daylight. Indeed you did it secretly, but I will do this thing before all Israel, and under the sun."

David's failure to discipline his children ought to motivate us to live rightly so we can not only leave a good example, but also be able to have clear enough consciences to discipline our own children while there is yet time.

Withholding a Knowledge of God

Withholding a knowledge of—and love for—God is the greatest form of child abuse perpetuated on our children. Some parents will say, "I'm going to allow my children to make up their own mind about religion. I don't think I have the right to impose my particular religious beliefs on them."

My response to this prattle is, "Poppycock!" That is plain foolishness. We teach our children to brush their teeth. We make them eat their vegetables before they are allowed dessert. If they are overweight, we feed them less fattening foods, and if they are not eating we take them to the doctor. And we make them wear a coat outdoors on a snowy day. As parents we have a broader view of life and of what is important. Children are immature and do not know what is best for them. That is why we are responsible to train our children in the things of God and introduce them, at the youngest age possible, to the knowledge of God.

In Deuteronomy 6:1-2 we read:

> Now this is the commandment, the statutes and the judgments which the LORD your God has commanded me to teach you, that you might do them in the land where you are going over to possess it, so that you and your son and your grandson might fear the LORD your God, to keep all His statutes and His commandments, which I command you, all the days of your life, and that your days may be prolonged.

The book of Deuteronomy also describes how and where we are to teach our children about God. I know a family who had a child who begged to go to church. The little boy would cry to go and learn about the Lord. The mother and father were disinterested and lazy. Each Sunday morning they would put the child off. "Perhaps next week we'll go," they said. But sadly, the next Sunday never came. As time went on the child's pleading became less frequent. Eventually the child lost interest in attending church. As the boy grew older and became more and more rebellious, the mother would ask him if he wanted to attend services. No more was there interest or desire in the young man's heart. The open door had been closed. The young boy is now a grown man in his forties. He never goes to church, and he treats his mother with hateful disrespect. There are many forms of abuse, but withholding a knowledge of God from a child is the most damning of them all.

Withholding Approval and Acceptance

How do we provoke our children to anger by withholding our approval from them? We exasperate them by showing them that no matter what they do, it is never enough. In the controversial book *Hillary's Choice* by Gail Sheehy, she tells about the life of Hillary Rodham Clinton, the wife of President Bill Clinton. What she documented was a sad story of a father who withheld his acceptance and the disastrous results:

> What is not known about her (Hillary Clinton) is that her father was a very punishing man. Tough, tobacco chewing, gruff, demanding, life was combat. And she did everything she could to please him. But she was unable to please him. He always kept the bar up— rising higher and higher and higher. "Well, you brought home straight A's. That must be a pretty easy school you went to." Welleseley College was anything but easy. And in 1969, when Hillary made history there as the only student ever to deliver the commencement address, Hugh Rodham didn't even come to hear his daughter speak. His dismissiveness had a dual effect—that Hillary became incredibly persistent, but in some ways deeply insecure.[3]

This attitude of pushing for more and more without giving approval for what has been accomplished produces angry, insecure, and hateful children. When an overweight child loses 10 pounds over a summer, do we ask her why didn't she lose more? When our children live with unattainable expectations from their parents, they lose heart.

Haim Ginott wrote:

> A child learns what he lives. If he lives with criticism he does not learn responsibility. He learns to condemn himself and to find fault with others. He learns to doubt his own judgment, to disparage his own ability, and to distrust the intentions of others. And above all, he learns to live with continual expectation of impending doom.[4]

God shows us great love and acceptance, despite our shortcomings and failures. It is our responsibility to offer this same attitude toward our children. When we get to heaven there won't be a one of us who will hear, "Best done, good and faithful servant." No, our very best effort will only get a "Well done." None of us do it all right. There is only One who was perfect, and His children constantly fail.

Withholding Affection

We hear a lot of different ideas about what "love" really is. For a true definition of the word, most of us know to go to the passage in 1 Corinthians 13: "Love is patient, love is kind, and is not jealous; love does not brag and is not arrogant, does not act unbecomingly; it does not seek its own, is not provoked, does not take into account a wrong suffered" (verses 4-5).

It is easy, and even tempting, to use this passage as a gauge for whether or not our children are acting in a loving manner. Instead, this text should be used as a mirror for moms to help us to see if we are the ones behaving in a loving way toward our children. This is necessary because it is so often the lack of godly love and affection that can lead children into angry attitudes and lifestyles.

First of all, **love is patient**. Why is it that kids seem to never want to ask questions until the phone rings? If the answer to this question could be found, so could the cure for the common cold! The literal meaning of the word "patient" is "long-tempered." It is most commonly referred to being patient with people, rather than being patient with circumstances or happenings. Love practiced does not fly off the handle, strike out at the object of the irritation, and seek revenge when repentance is not quickly achieved. Ecclesiastes 7:8 says, "Patience of spirit is better than haughtiness of spirit." Love is not easy, but it is patient.

Love is kind. While patience indicates suffering through someone else's irritating behavior, kindness requires us to give goodness back in its place. It is not enough to endure patiently the immature actions of our children, but we must go to the next step in returning kindness. When a child spills his milk, patience demands us to recognize the action was not intentional but merely a byproduct of not having the dexterity of mature hands. Kindness, on the other hand, obligates us to respond not with jerked and irritating gestures, but with understanding.

Proverbs 31:26 says, "She opens her mouth in wisdom, and the teaching of kindness is on her tongue." I want to have the attitude of sweetness that is demonstrated in Isaiah 40:11 when God is speaking concerning those He loves: "Like a shepherd...He will gently lead the nursing ewes." Kindness is not just a feeling; it is an action of goodness.

Love is not jealous. The two previous descriptions of love have shown us what love *is*. Love is patient and it is kind. Now, we see what love is *not*. It is not jealous. Love and jealousy cannot coexist, because they are opposite each other. Are we showing a controlling, dominating, resentful, form of anger called jealousy toward our children? The same damage that jealousy can do in our marriages—and the ungodly attitudes it fosters—is equally destructive in our relationships with our kids. There are loving boundaries we need to establish with our children, but a controlling, dominating spirit crushes them and provokes them to anger.

Love does not brag. I have found myself at times bragging about my children to other people. Sometimes my braggadocio is born out of a clean motive, where I genuinely am grateful for how God has gifted and blessed my son and daughter. But, if I am honest, there are times when my public bragging over some honor they have been presented or some opportunity they have been afforded is unclean. At those times, my words are delivered for the self-serving purpose of demonstrating what a wonderful job I think I've done in raising them. Bragging can not only be a selfish act on the part of the parent, but it can also put an enormous and unnecessary amount of pressure on the child.

I recall talking to a mother who saw firsthand the harm that can be done as a result of bragging about a child. She was telling a group of people about what a blessing her son had been to her and her husband. She pointed out the many achievements he had enjoyed and just how much she loved him and was proud of him. The mother honestly thought she was doing him good by flattering him in such a public way.

The son sadly looked at her and said, "Mom, I'm not as good as you think I am."

Unknown to the mother, her son was struggling with some very deep issues in his life. Her public bragging put pressure on him to perform. This was something that he could not withstand. She thought she was building him up, but doing so in a public forum only brought to light his sense of failure and his inability to live up to her unrealistic expectations and praise. There is a godly place where we can affirm our children. We can build them up in a good way, always pointing to the goodness of God as the source of any virtue in us and them. It would seem the difference between bragging and affirming words would be in putting the glory in flesh, rather than in God who deserves all adoration and praise.

We have a generation of children who are very frustrated because they have been told that they can do or be "anything." When they get out into the real world, they find that this is an unrealistic expectation. In fact, telling our children that they can do anything is *not* the right message. We should be encouraging our children to seek what God wants them to do and to pursue that high goal. Taking the emphasis off their own talents and abilities and spotlighting God's ultimate desire to use them in the way He sees fit will direct them in the right path.

Ultimately, we should instruct our children that the only place any of us can boast is in the cross and what Christ has done for us. For some reason I used to think it was all right to brag if it wasn't bragging about myself. Now I see that bragging is giving a person a place that only God is worthy to hold. Philippians 3:7-8 says, "But whatever things were gain to me, those things I have counted as loss for the sake of Christ. More than that, I count all things to be loss in view of the surpassing value of knowing Christ Jesus my Lord, for whom I have suffered the loss of all things, and count them but rubbish in order that I may gain Christ."

Love is not arrogant. The more I study what real love is, the more I see my failings as a mother. I must be honest with you—this is becoming more and more painful for me as I see how I may have provoked my children by displaying an attitude of arrogance. Even though my parental role seems to be scripturally built on the superiority of the parent and the subordination of the child, using a spirit of arrogance on our children will only provoke them to anger. The chain of command is given clearly in Colossians 3:18-21, and yet love must govern all aspects of our relationships. Love is not arrogant. Children truly do react to the arrogance that provokes. In Proverbs 8:13 God tells us what He thinks of arrogance: "The fear of the LORD is to hate evil; pride and arrogance and the evil way, and the perverted mouth, I hate."

As I read these passages, I wonder how many conflicts were brought on between me and my children—not because they were rebellious as I had previously thought, but as a result of my know-it-all arrogance. And it helps to be able to recognize this foul attitude. It usually shows itself when my hands go to my hips and I take a military-type stance and spout out things like, "As long as you live under my roof, you'll do things my way!"

Love does not act unbecomingly. Miss Manners would be very pleased to find that love is not rude or does not display poor conduct; love is courteous. Perhaps if we as family members would treat each other with common courtesy—much like the way we treat the person bagging our groceries at the supermarket or a rank stranger in the department store—many of our problems could be solved.

An attitude of rudeness and a lack of manners toward those we love, specifically our children, reveal a sloppy heart. The common courtesies, the polite responses we use when responding to one another, defuse anger.

Love does not seek its own. Love is not selfish. This is most likely the key to all the problems in our lives, especially in regard to those we love. Putting ourselves above all others is the sin as old as the "garden."

Love is not easily provoked. When a person is interested in always getting his or her own way, the end result will be a person who is easily provoked. Why would this be the case? Because in this world, no one "has it their way" all the time. The truth be known, there will always be people and circumstances who stand in the way of us getting our own way. Ofttimes, it is our children who end up thwarting our best-laid plans. Because of this, they often become the objects of our anger.

Love doesn't keep record of a wrong suffered. The phrase "keep record" in the Greek means to keep a ledger. *Logizomai* is a bookkeeper's term which indicates to occupy oneself with calculations, to keep tabs, to put one's account either in his favor or against him. How does this unloving attitude affect our relationship with our children? Instead of raking up wrongs done, we are to be in the process of dealing with the wrong, forgiving the offense, and ultimately covering it with love. First Peter 4:8 is a wonderful reminder to us as mothers: "Above all, keep fervent in your love for one another, because love covers a multitude of sins."

When our mirror reflects 1 Corinthians 13, then we will be giving our children what they need in order to avoid the consuming power of anger.

Withholding Mercy

Regardless of which side you stand on, either being in the need of mercy or being the one who gives it, when it is withheld, there is no rest. Proverbs 3:3-4 says, "Let not mercy and truth forsake thee: bind them about thy neck; write them upon the table of thine heart; so shalt thou find favour and good understanding in the sight of God and man" (KJV).

I find it interesting that mercy and truth are linked together in this passage. When it comes to being a mom, these two virtues have many opportunities to be displayed. One reason is that no one knows the truth about one's child the way a mother does. How many of us have walked into a room only to discover our kid doing something that leaves us completely shocked? At that moment, when truth is in its rawest form, we have to make a choice between judgment or mercy. Love demands we choose mercy. After all, look what God did for all of us on the Cross!

Withholding Our Presence

My friend Melissa was confused as to why she was having such a difficult time with her three-year-old daughter. "I'm at my wit's end," she told me, "and I just can't handle her. I bought her some new pants, since she had outgrown her old ones. I knew she is very picky about how her clothes look and fit, so we tried the pants on and she agreed that they were fine. I took off the tags, washed them, and had them ready for her to wear the next day. When it was time for her to get ready for the babysitter, she would not put the pants on and pitched a fit complaining that they hurt her around her waist. She screamed until I couldn't take it anymore."

After talking to Melissa and asking how her daughter responded to other people in her life, it was clear the only person the little girl refused to cooperate with was her mother. I responded, "I wonder if there could be something that your daughter is angry with you about?" As we talked through the situation, some things were made clear.

First of all, the daughter is not a "morning person." She wakes up grumpy until she has time to get fully alert. What seemed to be happening in the mornings, I discovered, was that the mother wanted to give her daughter as much time to sleep as possible and waited until the last minute to wake her. As a result, she was abruptly waking her little one and immediately telling her to put her clothes on. The daughter would then respond with resistance. The more the child protested, the more the mother pushed so she could get to work on time. The fight was repeated every morning.

I asked Melissa how the child responded to the babysitter. "Oh, she'll listen to her; it's me she won't obey." As we talked, I came to believe the little girl was angry at her mother for leaving her all day long. The first thing the child heard each morning was, "Hurry up and get dressed so I can take you to the sitter." I asked the mom if she ever told her daughter how sad it made her to leave her all day. I suggested, "You think you're doing what you must so you can provide the things you want your daughter to have, but all she knows is that you can't wait to get her to the sitter and leave her there."

Of course, after the raging fights each morning, the mother was glad to be free of the child's defiance. She didn't hate her daughter, but she did hate the conflicts each day. The morning scenes left both mother and child unhappy and frustrated. What a vicious cycle! The more the mother pushed, the more the child felt rejected and unloved, and the more anger she expressed.

We expect children to think like adults, and we excuse adults who act like children. The child was being "dropped" by accident. The little girl wanted her mother, and she felt she was being left all alone. The end result was that she was provoked to anger.

I wish I could tell you that the mother quit her job and started staying home with the girl. Unfortunately, that is not what happened, and the anger continues. We live in a society that has sanctioned hiring others to raise our children. Our absence has left a generation feeling unloved and unwanted. Is it any wonder that the young are angry and expressing that anger in the most shocking ways? One person even said, "Boys don't cry tears, they cry bullets!"

Withholding Forgiveness

In the beginning pages of this book I chronicled my own personal need to forgive. Since our children have imperfect parents, there is no question that they too must learn to do the same. Our children will learn to pardon others as they watch us deal with the hurts and offenses that come our way.

When we—the parents—harbor bitterness and resentment toward others, we are teaching our children to be hurtful and hurt-filled individuals. We cheat them out of one of the basic tools of productive Christian living when we do not offer them the living example of a continual "forgiver."

As parents we are to offer some guidelines on how to forgive. The Word of God is the beginning and ending resource on the subject. Romans 12:17-21 says:

> Never pay back evil for evil to anyone. Respect what
> is right in the sight of all men. If possible, so far as it
> depends on you, be at peace with all men. Never take
> your own revenge, beloved, but leave room for the
> wrath of God, for it is written, "Vengeance is Mine, I will
> repay," says the Lord. "But if your enemy is hungry, feed
> him, and if he is thirsty, give him a drink; for in so doing
> you will heap burning coals upon his head." Do not be
> overcome by evil, but overcome evil with good.

One of the greatest spiritual blessings I have given my children has been forgiving my childhood offender and thus being able to more fully understand the power and the blessing of forgiveness. My mother inspired me in this area on the last day of her life.

Prior to learning that she was seriously ill, Mom had been feeling all right but noticed she was losing weight. After having six children and reaching middle age, she was about 50 pounds larger than she was in her younger years. Since she was healthy and strong, her extra weight did not bother her. When she told her doctor that she was concerned about the weight loss, he dismissed her observation. The doctor was an avid runner and had always been a bit bothered by Mom's lack of concern for her added poundage. When she brought up the weight loss, he replied, "Good. It's about time you took off those pounds." Mom informed him that she was not dieting and she had no explanation for the loss. He ignored her anxiety.

Each time over the next year when her weight showed a decline, her doctor saw no need to investigate the cause. Finally, after a family member became more concerned, she insisted he find the reason for the weight changes. Within a few days, it was discovered that Mom had cancer and had been sick for a couple of years.

I can't tell you how upset Mom was with her doctor. His arrogant, know-it-all attitude had prevented him from giving her the timely care that she deserved. By the time the cancer was discovered, it was all through her body.

Mom was one of those patients who responded very well to chemotherapy. For the following 10 years she battled the cancer and received her treatments. She became increasingly bitter toward the doctor, whom she blamed for the cancer being so advanced when it was discovered. Anyone who tried to talk to her about forgiving the doctor was met with a deaf ear. The loss of her health was so hard for her to bear that she was not open to discussing it.

On Mom's last day of life, when my father and sister took her to the emergency room, you could never guess who the admitting doctor was. Yes, the neglectful, offending physician who Mom so fiercely blamed for her health problems was the one who was to examine her and admit her into the hospital. No doubt it was a divine encounter, one that I am sure was orchestrated by God Himself. Confronted with the last few hours of my mother's life, the doctor apologized, and Mom forgave him. There was great rejoicing among those who loved Mom and wanted her to enjoy the peace of God that passes all understanding, especially in her final hours.

Forgiveness sets us free from our offender. What a great gift we can give our children as we forgive those who have hurt us, and as we ask forgiveness of those we have harmed. Withholding the example of forgiveness will eventually provoke our children to anger.

Withholding Necessities

When I was a young child I rode a bus to school 10 miles each way. I recall that one particular family, whose children rode my bus, was very impoverished. Those children suffered ridicule and teasing because they smelled so badly. Actually, each morning as they waited for the bus to arrive, they would eat the wild onions that grew by the side of the road. Consequently, when they entered the bus, so did the aroma of their less-than-tantalizing breakfast. I always felt so sorry for them because I knew it wasn't their fault that they were so poor.

The parents were sad cases as well. However, it wasn't that they had so little money, but it was how they chose to spend their limited resources. They had plenty of money for cigarettes and liquor, but none for soap, toothpaste, and deodorant. The children were teased and taunted, and they were extremely angry children. Their parents did not live by the precepts found in 2 Corinthians 12:14, which reads, "Here for the third time I am ready to come to you, and I will not be a burden to you; for I do not seek what is yours, but you; *for children are not responsible to save up for their parents, but parents for their children*" (emphasis mine). Proverbs 19:14 reminds us, "House and wealth are an inheritance from fathers." And Proverbs 13:22 says, "A good man leaves an inheritance to his children's children."

We have a responsibility to provide for our children the material possessions that they need. This is not to say we are supposed to buy them $200 tennis shoes, give them a new car when they turn 16, or provide an Ivy League college experience. However, God has given us the job of providing for our children the necessities of life.

When there is a needed resource that seems out of reach for the parents to provide, it is a spiritual blessing to go to the heavenly Father and make our request known. Our children will learn to depend on God as they watch us depend on Him.

It is my hope that your children will avoid anger as a result of your careful attempt to not withhold what they really need. One thing is for sure: The harder you work at raising children who know the joy of a godly example, the happier Mama will be!

12

Removing the Fuse from Explosive Anger

"...take courage; I have overcome the world."

—John 16:33

When I was much younger and not quite as smart, I would join my friends on the Fourth of July as we handled—and mishandled—firecrackers. These little devices are designed to give great pleasure to children, as well as completely rattle the adults within earshot. Little did I know all those years ago that in our cheap paper and powder thrills was a picture that shows the very solution to controlling fits of rage. You may think I am attempting to end this book with a "bang." However, you will discover the opposite is true!

There are basically three parts to a working firecracker. First, there is the tightly rolled paper containing a highly explosive charge. Second is the fuse. It is usually made of a long, slender piece of paper and covered with a less combustible coating. And third, in order to complete the thrill, there needs to be a source of fire in order to deliver a high enough level of heat to get the fuse started. Whether it was from a match or from an adult's cigarette lighter, once the spark began at the end of the fuse, we kids would jump up and run screaming in anticipation of the noise that would soon follow. Over and over again, until the yard was littered with debris, my friends and I would enjoy the commotion we managed to cause in the community.

What I want to focus on is the link—or the fuse—that stands between the outside source of combustion and the combustible material. Regardless of the power and vulnerability of the charge—or the intensity of the spark—if there is no fuse to deliver the heat, there will not be an explosion.

I can remember very well the excitement I felt when I would hold one of those firecrackers as a kid. I also recall how easy it was to pull the fuse out of the main body of the little bomb. As I look back on it now, I realize that when I did, I completely disarmed the device. Without the necessary connection, it was void of providing a thrill.

I have a feeling that by now you are starting to see the picture I want to draw regarding the anger issue. As we recognize our propensity to go off into outbursts of anger, as well as realize there will always be those ever-present "sparks" of irritation, it behooves us then to find a way to remove the fuse that would link the two sources. In the same way I've done throughout this book, I ask now: Is pulling the fuse out of anger as simple as removing the little paper igniter out of a youngster's firecracker? You can be sure it is not. It may be simple, but it's not easy!

How do we do it? How do we disconnect the very thing that Satan often uses to send fire to the deadly load of emotional powder that waits for a spark? I hope to answer that question by telling you about a concept from the Scriptures. This teaching is an adaptation of a sermon that came from the heart of Jeff Wickwire, a great pastor and teacher in Fort Worth, Texas. His wealth of insight on a passage in the book of Jeremiah holds incredible hope for those of us who want to "remove the fuse."

In the first four verses of chapter 12, we find Jeremiah crying out to God. Jeremiah had been placed in the unenviable position of pronouncing judgment on the very people he grew up with and loved very much. Striving to be obedient to God, the lamenting Jeremiah spoke forth the words the Lord had given him to say. He told his countrymen that God was going to judge them, even though the other prophets gave false hope to the people and told them they would suffer no harm. What was Jeremiah's reward for truthful and faithful service to the word he was given from God? His friends and family wanted to kill him. And to make matters worse, there was no evidence that God was bringing forth His wrath on the people as the prophet had predicted. To the contrary, the very people on whom the pronounced judgment was given were actually prospering and doing well. Jeremiah was not only upset with God, but he was also completely confused.

Looking at the predicament Jeremiah faced, I can only imagine how angry I would have been if I were in his sandals. His friends and family were plotting against him, even to take his life. He couldn't trust anyone to be truthful and honest with him even though he was serving God through obedience. He didn't understand why things were not turning out the way the Lord promised.

It was around the year 600 B.C. when Jeremiah went to God asking Him to explain what was going on. Amazingly enough, the admonition God gave him over 2,400 years ago is the very truth that helped me pull the fuse out of the bomb of anger just recently. What could God have possibly said to Jeremiah that would help me disarm my explosive temper—something I did while standing in a grocery line? Read on!

In light of the confusion the faithful prophet was experiencing, God spoke to him and said, "If you have run with footmen and they have tired you out, then how will you compete with horses? If you fall down in a land of peace, how will you do in the thicket of the Jordan?"

Before I get to the supermarket story, let me explain the significance of this verse as it pertains to managing anger. What was God saying to Jeremiah when He warned him concerning being wearied by footmen? As I understand, in the strategy of war the first and most easily defeated of the fighting ranks was the initial wave of men who approached on foot. After these warriors did as much damage to the enemy as they could, then the generals would send in the cavalry, or the horsemen, to continue the battle. The horsemen were much more formidable competitors, with not only the use of their weapons at their disposal, but also the advantage of the strength of the horses. After the horsemen accomplished their destructive chore, then the final warriors would come to fight. They were the charioteers, and their responsibility was to finish the job and, of course, take credit for the victory.

If there was any hope for triumph, the opponent had to first defeat the footmen, then the horsemen, and ultimately the charioteers. God continued to admonish Jeremiah with another illustration from his everyday life. The Lord said to the prophet, "If you fall down in a land of peace, how will you do in the thicket of the Jordan?" To explain just what Jeremiah was being told, consider this actuality. Every year in the Middle East, the rains would come and flood the banks of the Jordan River. As a result, rich deposits were left in the soil and thick vegetation would grow up along the shore and amongst the thicket. It was in these jungles of the Jordan that the lions and other wild animals would live. God was saying to Jeremiah, "If you can't withstand the verbal attacks of your own hometown where you live in relative peace, how will you survive the lions of the Jordan? What God was apparently saying to His prophet was not easy to hear: "Toughen up!" The Lord wanted Jeremiah to realize that the struggles he was facing with his own people were mere "footmen" compared to what was coming. If he let the small things (people complaining about him and talking behind his back) bring him down, how could he ever cope when the greater trials and tests came?

Our lives are filled with "footmen" who are irritating and inconvenient. But we must ask ourselves the same question that Jeremiah faced. If we can't deal effectively with the small irritations, what's going to happen when really hard times come our way?

This life-changing challenge rescued me from allowing the fires of hell to ignite the fuse to explosive and embarrassing anger not too long ago. As I mentioned earlier, it happened at the grocery store. A situation suddenly arose that brought to light the key to removing the fuse to rage. I was waiting in line at an extremely busy time of the day. The checkout clerk was working at a noticeably slow pace. She was casually looking around the store and merrily conversing with her fellow "workers" (and I use the word *worker* lightly). It was as though she knew whether or not she hurried, she was going to be on the job till five o'clock in the afternoon.

As I observed her overly relaxed demeanor, I became more stressed and rushed with each passing moment. I immediately started getting agitated and irritable. In my mind I complained, "How dare she waste my time in such a selfish way?" Then I began to talk to myself, and that's never a good sign.

As the anger continued to rise, the picture in Jeremiah suddenly came to my mind. As I stood there glaring at the slothful woman, I could almost hear the footsteps of the ground soldiers as they ran across the battlefield in my heart. I realized the woman at the cash register was merely a *footman*. The truth that came rushing into my soul caused me to reassess the situation, and suddenly I found myself relaxing. My muscles lost their tenseness, and I could literally feel my blood pressure lower to a medically safe level. That's when it hit me. *I had removed the fuse!* The innocent woman had no idea that she had just been spared a blast from the bomb I had managed to disarm.

Ultimately, the truth of the matter came to me. *If standing in line at a grocery store and facing this lazy laborer can throw me into a tantrum, what am I going to do if something really bad happens?* I wondered.

By seeing the behavior of the clerk for what it really was (a small yet important test that was teaching me patience) everything changed. I started looking around, taking my time. I suddenly realized I was not the only person on the planet. I noticed the people who were waiting patiently in the other line. A few minutes before, they had just been a meaningless blur. Instead, they became individuals worth observing. By the time it was my turn to check out, I was not at all keyed up and my gut was no longer twisted. I was not popping medications for my spastic colon. How refreshing it was for me to realize that the clerk and all the other "footmen" I might encounter daily are fuses that can actually be removed. I was excited that I was finally learning this truth.

Jesus recognized the "footmen" in His life. Luke 9:51-56 says:

> And it came about, when the days were approaching for His ascension, that He resolutely set His face to go to Jerusalem; and He sent messengers on ahead of Him. And they went, and entered a village of the Samaritans, to make arrangements for Him. And they did not receive Him, because He was journeying with His face toward Jerusalem. And when His disciples James and John saw this, they said, "Lord, do You want us to command fire to come down from heaven and consume them?" But He turned and rebuked them, [and said, "You do not know what kind of spirit you are of; for the Son of Man did not come to destroy men's lives, but to save them."] And they went on to another village.

The disciples were upset because the Samaritans had disrespected Jesus. This offense stirred up anger in their hearts. What was their response to having someone reject their Master? They wanted to fry them. Jesus rebuked them, however. He knew the Samaritans were the "footmen" and that the "horsemen" (the Sanhedrin court), as well as the "charioteers" (the Cross), waited for Him in Jerusalem. He was not about to let something less important get him off-track.

What is the purpose of the "footmen" in our lives? They are meant to toughen us up so we can endure the "horsemen" and the "charioteers." And it's not a matter of *if* they approach—it's *when*! In John 16:33 we are promised trouble: "In this world you will have tribulation, but take heart! I have overcome the world" (NIV). We love the promises of God. We memorize them and even quote them as though we are blackmailing God to do us good. I've even heard people pray, "Now, God, You promised that You would meet all of my needs according to Your riches in Christ Jesus. God, I need some of those riches right now, and I'm holding You to Your word. Give me my stuff." But not too many of us like the promise of tribulation found in the above-mentioned text. Most of us would just as soon skip over this passage.

What do we do, then, with the "footmen" that have the potential, like a fuse, to ignite our anger and trouble our peaceful existence? To answer that question, go with me to James 1:2-3: "Consider it all joy, my brethren, when you encounter various trials [footmen], knowing that the testing of your faith produces endurance." First, notice that the text says *when*, not *if*. It is with certainty that the footmen will come.

Second, look at the phrase "consider it all joy." The Greek word for "consider" is *hegeomai,* which is a command, an imperative. It does not come naturally for us to look on trials, troubles, challenges and the like with a sense of elation. In different commentaries this phrase indicates pure, unmixed, complete, or total joy. How could we possibly see the testing and troubles that we encounter as "joyful" things? We can only see them as joyful if we look past the problem and see the result of letting God have His perfecting way in us.

Thirdly, consider the word "encounter." The Greek for this is *peripipto,* which has the literal idea of "falling into it." This may describe an unexpected experience illustrated by the man in Luke 10:30 who fell among robbers. Life is filled with the interruptions and explosions that rock our world unexpectedly. What is our response supposed to be to these incidences in our lives? We are to face them with complete, utter joy, knowing that the end result will produce endurance.

Now we come to the phrase, "the testing of your faith." In this challenging excerpt is the word "testing." It is important for us to understand that being tested is not the same as being tempted. I mention this because I have heard too many of us interchange these two words. By doing so we miss an important point. The Greek word for "testing," found in verse 3 of the text, is very interesting. It is the word *dokimion.* It indicates that the test is to prove we are good and acceptable, to show that we are faithful. Farther down in the passage, however, in verse 13, James uses the word "tempted." The difference between the two words is significant.

The Greek word for "tempted" is *perirazo.* It refers to soliciting someone to sin. While God tests us in order to produce endurance, He never entices us to sin through temptations. That is the work of the devil. (Consider Satan's tempting of Christ in Matthew chapter 4.)

When trials come, we can be assured that if God allowed them through His filter of love, then they are to produce good in us. Hebrews 12:11 says: "All discipline for the moment seems not to be joyful [at the time it feels like a charioteer], but sorrowful; yet to those who have been trained by it, afterwards it yields the peaceful fruit of righteousness [when we see the good the testing yielded we realize it was a footman]."

Getting back to the grocery store scene, I have to admit I left there feeling encouraged in my innermost being. I had faced the test and successfully disconnected the fuse by dealing with the "foot-lady." As a result I spared myself, as well as some innocent bystanders, the shrapnel of my ire. Having tasted victory, I don't want to go back to letting the battle be lost in its first stage. To win I must remember that the ground troops will inevitably show up, and will do so in many uniforms. For example, they'll be dressed like the inconsiderate driver (footman) who pulls in front of me on the interstate or my messy children (little footmen!) who unravel my spirit by dismantling my house. If I don't let these small irritations ignite the fuse, then I'll be better prepared when the horsemen, and eventually the charioteers, show up with their big guns. And as some of you know all too well, they do show up.

I hope this mixture of metaphors, the fuse, and the footmen, is helpful in giving you a way of escape from the destructive explosions of anger that you long to avoid. And I hope the journey you have taken with me on the road *from* rage has led you to the Prince of Peace. If so, the writing of this book was worth the effort. I will admit, by the way, that it was simple to tell about the terrible "thing" that happened to me as a child, but in no way was it easy. To dredge up those hurts only reminded me of how incredibly important it is to hug in and hold on to God, to let Him clean out the lint trap of anger, to bridle my tongue, to let Him help me disarm the bomb, and to let Christ win the anger game. This ongoing work in my heart—and now, I hope, in yours—will bless our spouses, our children, and our friends. More importantly, may it bring glory to the One—our Savior, Jesus Christ—whom we can count on to be the Victor over the charioteers of our lives.

Notes

Chapter 2

1. Dr. Gary Chapman, *The Other Side of Love* (Chicago: Moody Press, 1999), p. 21.

Chapter 3

1. www.massnews.com/, Nov. 1999. Vol. 1, No. 6.
2. Annie Chapman, *What Do I Want?* (Pleasant View, TN: S&A Family, 1999), pp. 130–133.

Chapter 6

1. Archibald D. Hart, *Feeling Free* (Old Tappan, NJ: Fleming Revell, 1979), pp. 73–74.

Chapter 8

1. John W. Reed, Compiler, *1100 Illustrations from the Writings of D. L. Moody* (Grand Rapids: Baker Book House, 1996), p. 294.
2. Paul Lee Tan, *Encyclopedia of 7700 Illustrations* (Rockville, MD: Assurance Publishers, 1988), p. 7.

3. John MacArthur, *The John MacArthur New Testament Commentary on James* (Chicago: Moody Press, 1998), p. 152.

Chapter 9

1. Steve Chapman, Times & Seasons Music/BMI/1999.

Chapter 10

1. Steve Chapman, Dawn Treader Music.
2. Steve Chapman, Times & Seasons Music/BMI.

Chapter 11

1. *Webster's New Twentieth Century Dictionary Unabridged* (United States: William Collins & World Publishing Co., 1977 and 1975), p. 896.
2. Steve Chapman, Times & Seasons Music/BMI/1998.
3. www.msnbc.com/news/, Nov. 30, 1999, 340364.asp#BODY.
4. Haim Ginott, *Between Parent and Child* (New York, 1965), p. 72.

Other Harvest House Reading

Power of a Praying™ Wife
Stormie Omartian
In this longtime bestselling book, Stormie Omartian shares how you can develop a deeper relationship with your husband by praying for him. Packed with practical advice on praying for specific areas, including decision-making, fears, spiritual strength, and sexuality. You will discover the fulfilling marriage God intended for you.

Power of a Praying™ Parent
Stormie Omartian
Stormie offers 30 easy-to-read chapters that focus on specific areas of prayer for parents. This personal, practical guide will help you become a strong prayer warrior for your children.

Goodbye Is Not Forever
Amy George
Amy was a baby when the Soviet secret police condemned her father to Siberia. During World War II, she witnessed firsthand the horrors of Hitler's Germany, yet also saw evidence that God's grace was at work long before she knew Him.

Women Helping Women
Elyse Fitzpatrick and Carol Cornish
A resource for women who desire to help other women. Each major life issue is covered with a concise overview, a clear biblical perspective, and practical guidelines from experts. You will be encouraged as you discover how God's Word changes hearts.

Heart Hunger
Cindi McMenamin
You long to be loved, to be known, to be understood. But who can meet those needs and touch your heart at its deepest level? Only the One who is the Creator of hearts. *Heart Hunger* is an invitation for you to enjoy true intimacy with God...and to find yourself filled, satisfied, and longing no more.